An Analysis of

Hamid Dabashi's

Iran
A People Interrupted

Bryan R. Gibson

www.macat.com
info@macat.com

Cover illustration: Etienne Gilfillan

Cataloguing in Publication Data
A catalogue record for this book is available from the British Library.
Library of Congress Cataloguing-in-Publication Data is available upon request.

ISBN 978-1-912303-20-5 (hardback)
ISBN 978-1-912128-40-2 (paperback)
ISBN 978-1-912282-08-1 (e-book)

Notice
The information in this book is designed to orientate readers of the work under analysis,
to elucidate and contextualise its key ideas and themes, and to aid in the development
of critical thinking skills. It is not meant to be used, nor should it be used, as a
substitute for original thinking or in place of original writing or research. References and
notes are provided for informational purposes and their presence does not constitute
endorsement of the information or opinions therein. This book is presented solely for
educational purposes. It is sold on the understanding that the publisher is not engaged
to provide any scholarly advice. The publisher has made every effort to ensure that
this book is accurate and up-to-date, but makes no warranties or representations with
regard to the completeness or reliability of the information it contains. The information
and the opinions provided herein are not guaranteed or warranted to produce particular
results and may not be suitable for students of every ability. The publisher shall not be
liable for any loss, damage or disruption arising from any errors or omissions, or from
the use of this book, including, but not limited to, special, incidental, consequential or
other damages caused, or alleged to have been caused, directly or indirectly, by the
information contained within.

CONTENTS

THE MACAT LIBRARY

The Macat Library is a series of unique academic explorations of seminal works in the humanities and social sciences – books and papers that have had a significant and widely recognised impact on their disciplines. It has been created to serve as much more than just a summary of what lies between the covers of a great book. It illuminates and explores the influences on, ideas of, and impact of that book. Our goal is to offer a learning resource that encourages critical thinking and fosters a better, deeper understanding of important ideas.

Each publication is divided into three Sections: Influences, Ideas, and Impact. Each Section has four Modules. These explore every important facet of the work, and the responses to it.

This Section-Module structure makes a Macat Library book easy to use, but it has another important feature. Because each Macat book is written to the same format, it is possible (and encouraged!) to cross-reference multiple Macat books along the same lines of inquiry or research. This allows the reader to open up interesting interdisciplinary pathways.

To further aid your reading, lists of glossary terms and people mentioned are included at the end of this book (these are indicated by an asterisk [*] throughout) – as well as a list of works cited.

Macat has worked with the University of Cambridge to identify the elements of critical thinking and understand the ways in which six different skills combine to enable effective thinking.
Three allow us to fully understand a problem; three more give us the tools to solve it. Together, these six skills make up the **PACIER** model of critical thinking. They are:

ANALYSIS – understanding how an argument is built
EVALUATION – exploring the strengths and weaknesses of an argument
INTERPRETATION – understanding issues of meaning

CREATIVE THINKING – coming up with new ideas and fresh connections
PROBLEM-SOLVING – producing strong solutions
REASONING – creating strong arguments

To find out more, visit **WWW.MACAT.COM.**

CRITICAL THINKING AND *IRAN: A PEOPLE INTERRUPTED*

Primary critical thinking skill: ANALYSIS
Secondary critical thinking skill: REASONING

Hamid Dabashi's 2007 *Iran: A People Interrupted* is simultaneously subtle, passionate, polarizing and polemical. A concise account of Iranian history from the early 19th-century onward, Dabashi's book uses his incisive analytical skills as a basis for creating a persuasive argument against the views of Iran that predominate in the West.

In Dabashi's view, Western approaches to Iran have been colored time and time again by the assumption that it is somehow trapped between regressive 'tradition,' and progressive 'modernity.' The reality, he argues, is quite the opposite: Iran has its own distinctive ideology of modernity, which is nevertheless opposed to many Western ideals. In order to prove his point, Dabashi draws on a lifetime's experience of literary criticism to analyse the relationship between Iran's intellectual and political elites over two centuries.

His analysis provides the key evidence for his reasoning by teasing out the implicit assumptions that underly the texts and people he examines. Looking beneath the surface of the evidence, Dabashi finds – time and time again – the traces of a uniquely Iranian notion of modernity that is quite at odds with its Western counterpart.

ABOUT THE AUTHOR OF THE ORIGINAL WORK

Born in Iran in 1951, **Hamid Dabashi** is a prolific Iranian American scholar, sociologist, and postcolonialist writer who specializes in Islamic studies, history, and culture. A passionate political activist in his youth, Dabashi studied in the United States, but went home to take part in the Iranian Revolution of 1978–9, before completing a double PhD back in America in 1984. His books have been highly praised, though his views on a number of subjects, including Israel, have polarized opinions. He is currently a professor of Iranian studies and comparative literature at Columbia University.

ABOUT THE AUTHORS OF THE ANALYSIS

Dr Bryan Gibson holds a PhD in International History from the London School of Economics (LSE) and was a post- doctoral research fellow at the LSE's Centre for Diplomacy and Strategy and an instructor on Middle Eastern politics in the LSE's Department of International History and the University of East Anglia's Department of Political, Social and International Studies (PSI). He is currently on the faculty of Johns Hopkins University and is the author of *Sold Out? US Foreign Policy, Iraq, the Kurds and the Cold War* (Palgrave Macmillan, 2015).

ABOUT MACAT

GREAT WORKS FOR CRITICAL THINKING

Macat is focused on making the ideas of the world's great thinkers accessible and comprehensible to everybody, everywhere, in ways that promote the development of enhanced critical thinking skills.

It works with leading academics from the world's top universities to produce new analyses that focus on the ideas and the impact of the most influential works ever written across a wide variety of academic disciplines. Each of the works that sit at the heart of its growing library is an enduring example of great thinking. But by setting them in context – and looking at the influences that shaped their authors, as well as the responses they provoked – Macat encourages readers to look at these classics and game-changers with fresh eyes. Readers learn to think, engage and challenge their ideas, rather than simply accepting them.

WAYS IN TO THE TEXT

KEY POINTS

- Hamid Dabashi is an Iranian American professor and literary critic at Columbia University in New York, and a political commentator for the news network Al Jazeera.

- In his book *Iran: A People Interrupted*, Dabashi weaves together 200 years of Iranian literature, history, and politics to illustrate the Iranian people's struggle against foreign imperialism*—the policy of empire building—and internal tyranny.

- Iran is at the forefront of international affairs, making Dabashi's analysis valuable to anyone interested in understanding why Iranians think and act as they do.

Who Is Hamid Dabashi?

Hamid Dabashi, the author of *Iran: A People Interrupted* (2007), was born in 1951 in Ahvaz, Iran, into a working-class family. His devout Muslim mother was a homemaker and herbalist who entertained the family with storytelling, while his father was a railroad laborer, toymaker, and talented cook.

Dabashi received his early education near home before moving to the Iranian capital, Tehran, to begin his university studies in August 1970. As a student he was a social activist and Iranian nationalist (that is, his patriotism shaped many of his political beliefs). He attended secret poetry readings and sought out subversive materials while avoiding the watchful eye of Iran's secret police, the SAVAK.*

Dabashi speaks openly of his childhood in *Iran: A People Interrupted*, including many personal stories of growing up during the reign of the Shah (king), Mohammad Reza Pahlavi.* He also shares his experiences of the aftermath of the Iranian Revolution* of 1978–9, in which the Shah was overthrown and the nation became an Islamic republic headed by a religious leader, the Ayatollah* Khomeini,* destroying Dabashi's hopes for a more democratic Iran.

After his undergraduate degree, Dabashi moved to the United States to study at the University of Pennsylvania. For his 1984 PhD in Sociology of Culture and Islamic Studies,* he wrote a thesis on the German sociologist Max Weber's* theory of charismatic authority*—a theory that explains the devotion we offer to particularly notable people. He followed this with a postdoctoral fellowship at Harvard University. He is now an American citizen and lives in New York City, where he is Hagop Kevorkian Professor of Iranian Studies and Comparative Literature at Columbia University. He lectures at universities around the world and is an outspoken political commentator for the global news organization Al Jazeera.

What Does *Iran: A People Interrupted* Say?

Interrupted is a history of intellectual and political life in Iran told through an examination of its philosophy and literature. Dabashi weaves together 200 years of Iranian writing and debate into a study of the people's struggle against foreign imperialism (mainly from Britain, Russia, and the United States) and homegrown tyranny (from the monarchy and religious leaders).

Dabashi uses a wide range of sources—poetry, cinema, political commentary, plus his own experiences and opinions—to illustrate Iran's rich artistic heritage and defiant national psyche. *Interrupted* reveals how generations of Iranian writers waged an intellectual battle against the forces of oppression. Dabashi's mission is to explode the Western myth that Iranian and other Middle Eastern societies are simply trapped between tradition* and the enlightened values associated with modernity.* He seeks to persuade people away from the "clichéd categorization of Iran as a country caught between a belligerent tradition and an alien modernity, and to adopt a more historically nuanced, culturally multifaceted, and materially grounded reading of Iran."[1]

Dabashi's central argument is that Iran's main ideology is one of anti-colonial modernity—in other words, that modern life is arranged on Iran's own terms rather than those of a foreign power. This attitude evolved naturally over two centuries of interaction between Iranian intellectuals in the arts and public life. Iran's intellectual mix, argues Dabashi, includes ideas imported from Europe during the artistic and cultural movement of the late seventeenth and eighteenth centuries known as the Enlightenment.* These ideas valued reason and liberty above tradition, championing representative democracy* (a system of government in which citizens elect people to represent them in state institutions that govern on their behalf) and civil disobedience* (the refusal to comply with laws or government orders as a form of protest).

Dabashi opens *Interrupted* with a scathing critique of leading scholars of foreign relations and international relations theory, whom he accuses of being "dead wrong" in their approach to history. He announces his intention to write "people back into the history of their regional and global resistance."[2] He then turns to a discussion of the famous Persian poet known as Sa'di,* who was an influence on Enlightenment thinking. Thinkers such as the French essayist Voltaire,*the German literary figure Johann Wolfgang von Goethe,* and even the American statesman and scientist Benjamin Franklin* were inspired by Sa'di's themes of freedom and justice. More importantly, Dabashi shows the poet's influence on the American poet and essayist Henry David Thoreau,* who developed the concept of civil disobedience. *Interrupted* charts how the natural inclination of Iranians to oppose domination and oppression influenced the heart of the European intellectual tradition.

According to Dabashi, the philosophical foundations laid by Sa'di and the importing of radical Enlightenment literature explain the origins of Iran's fundamental opposition to imperialism and its natural inclination to resist suppression from both internal and external sources. He develops these themes through a chronological analysis of four distinct periods of modern Iranian history. These are the Constitutional Revolution (1905–11),* in which the people of Iran successfully demanded governmental reforms; the Pahlavi dynasty (1925–79);* the Iranian Revolution (1978–9),* in which the ruling Pahlavi dynasty was overthrown; and the Islamic Republic* (1980 to present), in which a government founded on religious principles was instituted.

In each case, he shows how the writings of the age illustrate the Iranian people's fierce resistance to internal and external subjugation— and how it developed into a deep-seated anti-colonial ideology that persists to the modern day.

Why Does *Iran: A People Interrupted* Matter?
Hamid Dabashi began writing his controversial book in a New York still reeling from the 9/11* terrorist attacks on the city in 2001, in the course of which the city lost the twin towers of the World Trade Center when passenger jets were deliberately flown into them. President George W. Bush* condemned Iran as part of "an axis of evil"* that supported terrorism and therefore qualified as an enemy of the United States. Powerful voices in his administration called for military intervention in the Middle East over fears of weapons of mass destruction. In 2003 the United States led an invasion of Iraq, which shares a border with Iran. The battle of ideas in both academic and foreign policy circles was polarized between pro-intervention right-wing neoconservatives* on one side, who believed that American interests should be protected

through military force, and others, more politically moderate,* who favored non-military, diplomatic tactics on the other.

Dabashi's own view of the US political climate when he wrote *Interrupted* was that "villainous forces of fear and intimidation were reigning supreme."[3] In 2007 he presented an alternative view of his homeland, Iran. The text was the first history of its kind in the English language, and raised the fascinating question of whether literature can influence politics. In answer, Dabashi offers up the art of Iran as a sort of window into its soul.

Interrupted has relevance in an era when tensions in the Middle East continue to run high and Iran is seldom away from the international spotlight. The country's leadership changes, its controversial nuclear program,* and its uneasy relationship with the United States make Dabashi's text useful to those who want to understand the Iranian state of mind.

Dabashi is himself a polarizing voice in the debate over Iran, with *Interrupted* drawing both criticism and praise from his peers. It has been described as both "exasperating" and "arrogant," but also "complex" and "highly original." Whether students are delighted or enraged by *Interrupted*, there is no doubt that the text adds to our understanding of the Iranian people. It is, therefore, an invaluable guide for scholars, politicians, diplomats, and commentators who value its insights.

Interrupted is a major contribution to the study of Iran and helps explain many of Iran's actions today. It reveals a rich intellectual history that has long been centered on resisting internal and external suppression. It also underscores the intense sense of national pride shared by Iranians. These key characteristics become all the more important when considering the implications of negotiations over Iran's contentious nuclear program.

NOTES

1   Hamid Dabashi, *Iran: A People Interrupted* (New York: The New Press, 2007), 10.

2   Dabashi, *A People Interrupted*, 9.

3   Dabashi, *A People Interrupted*, xii.

SECTION 1
INFLUENCES

MODULE 1
THE AUTHOR AND THE
HISTORICAL CONTEXT

KEY POINTS

- *Iran: A People Interrupted* draws on Iranian literature, poetry, cinema, personal stories and political commentary to illustrate the people's long struggle against oppression.
- Hamid Dabashi's experience of the Iranian Revolution* that ousted a Shah (king) and installed an Ayatollah* (religious leader) played a significant role in shaping his writing.
- The text was written in the aftermath of the 9/11* terrorist attacks against America, at a time when United States President George W. Bush* and his advisors were openly hostile to Iran.

Why Read This Text?

Hamid Dabashi's *Iran: A People Interrupted* (2007) explores how the last 200 years of Iranian history can be understood through the work of its writers, poets, and politicians. Dabashi charts the long struggle by the Iranian people to resist imperialism* from abroad (that is, the interests of foreign empire-building nations) and tyranny at home, resulting in what he calls anti-colonial modernity.* By this he means a shared mindset that is homegrown rather than imposed by other countries such as Britain, Russia, or America. It evolved naturally through the interaction of intellectuals with the help of imported Enlightenment* ideas (that is, ideas arising from the intellectual movement of the seventeenth and eighteenth centuries that saw Europe adopt increasingly rational laws and social practices), including representative government* and democracy* (government by elections designed to reflect the wishes of

> **❝** The cosmopolitan culture that underlies much of Iranian history over the last two hundred years is neither entirely Islamic nor anti-Islamic, neither exclusively nationalist nor antinationalist, neither solely socialist nor antisocialist—and yet it is the dialectical culmination of all such political and ideological forces that come together to form its thick description of our moral and material history. **❞**
>
> Hamid Dabashi, *Iran: A People Interrupted*

the population) and civil disobedience* (a form of protest in which citizens refuse to obey certain laws or government orders).

Histories of Iran tend to focus on high-level politics, social activism, or religion. *Interrupted* stands out because Dabashi views history through the eyes of thinkers and writers—including himself. He weaves Iranian literature, poetry, cinema, political commentary, and his own personal stories together to illustrate how people have coped with various kinds of oppression.

Dabashi explains how Iran's blend of Shi'a Islam (or Shi'ism,* one of the two main branches of the Islamic faith), nationalism* (that is, politically expressed patriotism) and anti-imperialism* created a national ideology of resistance. Most Iranians are Shi'a Muslims and Islam is the basis of the country's law and government. Dabashi argues that modern Iranian thinking has its roots in Shi'a traditions of resistance and protest. These insights make *Interrupted* an important contribution to understanding both Iran's past and present.

Dabashi builds on the groundbreaking work of the Palestinian American literary theorist Edward Said,* his friend and colleague at Columbia University in New York. Said's book *Orientalism* argues that Western countries tend to see themselves as superior to other parts of the world they view as "exotic." Like Said, Dabashi uses *Interrupted* to challenge a group of "orientalist" scholars. He accuses them of inaccurately describing Iranian history and culture as a clash between "tradition"* and "modernity" and wrongly asserting that there is "a great insurmountable divide between Islam and the West."[1]

Author's Life

Dabashi was born into a working-class Muslim home in Ahvaz in Iran in 1951. His father was a railroad laborer and toymaker, his mother a homemaker and herbalist. Dabashi went to school in his home town before leaving to study at the University of Tehran in August 1970. As a student, Dabashi was a passionate nationalist and social activist, attending secret poetry readings and studying books considered subversive by the authorities. This was a dangerous way to live when Iran was ruled by the autocratic Shah (king) Mohammad Reza Pahlavi,* who had a secret police force (the SAVAK)* to weed out dissenters.

Dabashi lived through the Iranian Revolution of 1978–9 and this period of his life played a significant role in shaping *Interrupted*. The book is laced with Dabashi's experiences of living first under the Shah's reign and then in the Islamic state brought in by the revolution.

After his undergraduate degree, Dabashi was accepted into a doctoral program at the University of Pennsylvania and left Iran for the United States. He completed a dual PhD in Sociology of Culture and Islamic Studies in 1984, writing a thesis on Max Weber's* theory of charismatic authority*—the authority given to people on account of their heroism, say, or exceptional character, something he had witnessed firsthand in Iran. Dabashi won a post-doctoral fellowship at Harvard University, followed by a teaching post at Columbia University, New York, in 1988, where he is now Hagop Kevorkian Professor of Iranian Studies and Comparative Literature.

Author's Background

Interrupted was influenced by global events that Dabashi experienced firsthand. First was the Cold War,* a period of hostility between the communist* Soviet Union* and the United States from the late 1940s to the early 1990s. Iran was involved from the outset, as the Soviet Union refused to withdraw its troops from the country after World War II.* Iran took the matter—known as the Azerbaijan Crisis*—to the United Nations, which forced the Soviet Union to withdraw.

Iran became a battleground again in the early 1950s when popular prime minister Mohammad Mossadeq* nationalized the British-owned oil industry. The United States secretly intervened in 1953, overthrowing Mossadeq's government and allowing the Shah to rule as absolute monarch. From 1953 to 1979 he ruled Iran with an iron fist, seeking to transform his country from a deeply religious backwater into a modern regional power closely aligned with the West. In the 1960s he began the White Revolution,* a rapid modernization program along Western lines. But the Shah tried to liberalize his country while also continuing his authoritarian rule.

Opposition to his reign came to a head with an uprising in 1978. Police officials opened fire on a crowd during a protest, triggering a cycle of violence that ended in 1979 with the Shah fleeing the country and the birth of the Islamic Republic of Iran* led by Ayatollah Ruhollah Khomeini.* The revolution had a profound influence on the young Dabashi and, later, *Interrupted*. Taking a break from his studies in the US, he returned to Iran during the crisis to argue for representative democracy. Instead, the hardline religious authorities imposed a faith-based government that, like the Shah, violently suppressed opposition.

Another key influence was the aftermath of the terrorist attacks against the United States on September 11, 2001 (known as 9/11). Dabashi argues that the neoconservative* policymakers—politically right-wing thinkers who favored military intervention overseas— who surrounded President George W. Bush waged a campaign of fear and intimidation in order to reshape the world order to their designs. Dabashi made no effort to hide his disdain for the administration's policies towards Iran and the Middle East, especially the US-led invasion of Iraq,* which he described as "illegal and immoral."[2]

NOTES

1   Hamid Dabashi, *Iran: A People Interrupted* (New York: The New Press, 2007), 10.

2   Dabashi, *A People Interrupted*, 7.

ACADEMIC CONTEXT

KEY POINTS

- *Iran: A People Interrupted* falls within two broad academic fields: postcolonial studies* (inquiry into the various cultural and political legacies of colonialism)* and Iranian studies.

- Hamid Dabashi belongs to a school of thought that challenges how the brutal story of colonialism—settlement and usually rule by a foreign country—is told by Western scholars who use patronizing theories about non-European people.

- Dabashi was influenced by radical thinkers such as the French philosopher Jean-Paul Sartre,* but his main influence was his fellow Columbia University academic, the Palestinian American scholar Edward Said.*

The Work in its Context

Iran: A People Interrupted sits within two academic fields—Iranian studies and postcolonial studies.* Hamid Dabashi's work is part of an intellectual movement that challenges the way Western scholarship tends to reproduce misunderstandings of the "Orient" (especially the Middle East) and imply that the West is superior to other cultures.

Iranian studies include any topic related to Iran, and *Interrupted* deals directly with several aspects of the national experience over the last two centuries. These include history, politics, art, literature, and culture.

Interrupted also contributes to the academic debate around the effects of colonialism or imperialism*(being forced to accept foreign economic or political control)—or very often, both. This field tackles the long-term consequences, especially when the native population

> ❝ The disciplinary formation of 'Iranian studies' as a particularly potent component of 'Middle Eastern' and 'area studies' projects was a crucial factor in the narrative manufacturing of 'Iran.' If Orientalism ... was a manner of knowledge production conducive to European colonial domination over its 'Oriental' territories, the nationalist mode of knowledge production is equally instrumental in an illusively stabilized and historically fixed conception of a nation and its sealed boundaries. ❞
>
> Hamid Dabashi, *Iran: A People Interrupted*

has been exploited economically and prevented from developing a government of its own.

Dabashi shares the field's core concern over the politics of knowledge itself. That means understanding what the colonizing nation really knew about the people it subjugated and the relationship that developed between the colonizer and the colonized. Dabashi argues that patronizing colonial attitudes persist when Iran's past and present are presented as a simple battle between indigenous and backward-looking tradition* and Western-style modernity.*

Overview of the Field

Dabashi belongs to a school of postcolonialist scholars that includes the psychologist and philosopher Frantz Fanon,* the philosopher Jean-Paul Sartre, and the literary theorist and writer Edward Said. All have written extensively and highly critically about imperialism and decolonization* (the period between 1946 and 1975 when European imperial powers granted independence to their colonial possessions and the process by which a people addresses the cultural and political consequences of colonialism on its own terms). The first notable study of postcolonialism was Frantz Fanon's 1961 text, *Wretched of the Earth,*[1] a work that criticizes the dehumanizing effects of colonization and calls for it to end. Fanon's work instantly found support from the French philosopher Jean-Paul Sartre, who took the same approach to writing about France's colonial wars in North Africa in *Colonialism and Neocolonialism.*[2] These books helped to launch a method of critical analysis designed to expose and eliminate the effects of colonialism in Western literature.

In 1979, the literary theorist Edward Said picked up where Fanon and Sartre left off with *Orientalism,* a landmark critique of Western scholarship. Said condemned every Western study of the Middle East as not only biased but actually incapable of objective or productive scholarship. He was particularly angered by how Western academics portray Arab and Islamic culture as backward and being trapped between "tradition" and "modernity."[3] This critique firmly established postcolonial studies as a field of academic inquiry.

Academic Influences

Dabashi credits Fanon, Sartre, and Said with influencing his work. He also pays tribute to the works of the German social philosopher Jürgen Habermas;* the influential anthropologist Clifford Geertz,* noted for his works on cultural symbols; the founding sociologist Karl Mannheim;* and the German social theorist Max Weber.* Dabashi applied Weber's theory of charismatic authority* to the Prophet Mohammad,* the founder of the Islamic faith, for his doctoral thesis.

The chief academic influence on *Interrupted* remains Edward Said, however. As a junior colleague of Said at Columbia University, Dabashi shared his deep interest in the politics of the "Islamic" and the developing worlds. Dabashi was drawn to Said's critique of the essentially condescending nature of Western attitudes towards Middle Eastern, Asian, and North African societies. Said's influence on *Interrupted* is plain in Dabashi's use of the concept of Western orientalism*—a patronizing and exotic fiction of Asian and Middle Eastern culture—to unlock Iran's relations with the West over the past 200 years.

In this way Dabashi reveals a history far more complex than most studies of Iran imply. He says this is because of the tendency among orientalists such as the historian Bernard Lewis* to always depict the Middle East as being trapped between tradition and modernity. *Interrupted* uses Iran as a case study to challenge this well-worn version of events and to show how a national ideology of resistance developed over the course of 200 years of interaction with the West.

NOTES

1   Frantz Fanon, *Wretched of the Earth*, trans. Richard Philcox (New York: Grove Press, 2005).

2   Jean-Paul Sartre, *Colonialism and Neocolonialism*, trans. Azzedine Haddour (London: Routledge Classics, 2006).

3   Edward Said, *Orientalism* (New York: Vintage Books, 1979).

MODULE 3
THE PROBLEM

KEY POINTS

- *Iran: A People Interrupted* appeared in 2007 amid a raging debate over the direction of American foreign policy toward Iran following the apparent failure of the US-led Iraq War.*

- On one side were politically right-wing neoconservatives* who considered Iran part of "an axis of evil;"* on the other were liberals* calling for engagement and diplomacy.

- Hamid Dabashi fought passionately for the liberal position against the powerful voices around US President George W. Bush* pushing for the use of force against Iran.

Core Question

What is the truth about the Iranian people, their history, and their view of the world? Specifically, how have Iran's literary traditions influenced the creation of a national ideology that Hamid Dabashi calls "anti-colonial modernity"* (a modern political and social culture opposed to the influence of colonialism)?*

Iran: A People Interrupted is Dabashi's heartfelt answer as an Iranian in America and must be understood in the context of dramatic world events unfolding around him as he wrote. Academic battle lines were drawn after the 2001 terrorist attacks on the twin towers of the World Trade Center in New York (9/11)*—with anti-Iran neoconservative foreign-policy experts on one side and pro-diplomacy liberals on the other.

Dabashi opens *Interrupted* by saying he began writing in the aftermath of 9/11, an act of such savagery that it shook the American people to their core.[1] There was a culture of fear in the United States during the lead-up to the US-led invasion of Iraq* in March 2003. The world was left in no doubt about the United States' drive to

> **❝ I began writing this book during the darkest days of New York, in the aftermath of [9/11], when villainous forces of fear and intimidation were reigning supreme, seeking to silence dissent and interrupting the course of uplifting thoughts ... ❞**
>
> Hamid Dabashi, *Iran: A People Interrupted*

isolate Iran internationally when President George W. Bush labeled it as part of an "axis of evil." This compelled Dabashi to defend his homeland and present it in a different, more cosmopolitan, light.

The focus of *Interrupted* is the long struggle of the Iranian people against colonial imperialism* from Britain, Russia, and the United States, and the internal tyranny of royalty and the clergy. Dabashi does not present a traditional political history, exploring instead the relationship between Iran's writers and politicians over a 200-year period to show the complex, linked evolution of art, ideas, and politics.

The Participants

With *Interrupted*, Dabashi waded into a fierce intellectual debate between neoconservatives and liberals that had been raging since the 9/11 attacks on America. Neoconservatives favor promoting American interests around the world by encouraging a free-market economy and interventionist* foreign policy through military action, if they judge it necessary. Liberals challenged "neocon" foreign policy and orientalist* versions of history (that is, versions of history founded on a fiction of "the East" as primitive and exotic), arguing for working with other countries and restraint in the use of force.[2] The whole debate grew more heated in the lead-up to the US-led invasion of Iraq (Iran's neighbor) in 2003.*

Interrupted articulates Dabashi's undisguised loathing for what he describes as neoconservative, orientalist scholarship. He has "a bone to pick with these people, and all others like them, who have distorted the history of my people [Iranians] in order to belittle them and thus destroy their will to resist the regional domination of a predatory empire that these old and new con artists lucratively serve."[3] He singles out Kenneth Pollack,* a former Central Intelligence Agency* and National Security Council* analyst and Middle East scholar for special attention.

Pollack retired from government in 2001 and now works for the Brookings Institution,* a body offering advice and analysis on matters concerning global economics policy and international affairs. He has written several books on the region;[4] two proved highly controversial. One of these, *The Threatening Storm: The Case for Invading Iraq* (2002),[5] did exactly what its title suggests: it made the "case" for the US-led invasion of Iraq in 2003.* It is not surprising that Dabashi also took exception to his next book, *The Persian Puzzle: The Conflict Between Iran and America*.[6] This argued that the "United States no longer has the luxury of considering a purely passive approach to Tehran, nor can we simply wait for the Iranians to do something and then devise an ad hoc response. Iran is on the wrong path and marching down it quickly."[7]

Dabashi also takes issue with Iranian expatriates who agreed with the Bush administration's anti-Iranian message. These include Azar Nafisi* whose book *Reading Lolita in Tehran*[8] became a bestseller after being praised by neoconservative pundits. Nafisi, an Iranian-born professor of English literature, recounts her experiences living in Iran following the Iranian Revolution* when she invited female students to her home to discuss books. Her text was widely praised as a "rather wonderful book" that "touches a beauty of its own"[9] but Dabashi published an essay in 2006 that accused Nafisi of being a "native informer and colonial agent" of the American government. He said she denigrated Iran's culture of resistance to colonialism and catered to the "retrograde and reactionary forces" in the United States, who were painting Iran as the next target in the so-called War on Terror* (a military campaign conducted by the United States across many borders against individuals and groups believed to be orchestrating acts of terrorism).[10]

The Contemporary Debate

Dabashi is not afraid of engaging his contemporaries in argument over the political and philosophical questions of the day and can never be accused of sitting on the fence. Throughout *Interrupted* he makes explicit reference to a wide range of individuals that he either likes or intensely dislikes.

The book covers the sweep of Iranian history and Dabashi singles out people ranging from ancient Persian poets that he admires to modern scholars he despises. He makes no secret of the specific people or organizations that he disagrees with, including Pollack, Nafisi, and orientalist scholars such as the British American historian Bernard Lewis.*

Interrupted is also powered by Dabashi's confidence in his intellectual contribution to both scholarly understanding and public debate. In the introduction he insists that after finishing his book readers "will know more about Iran" than top American experts, both inside the government and throughout academia.[11]

At the same time, however, readers gain more from *Interrupted* if they have some wider knowledge of Iranian history, culture, and literature. They also benefit from reading Dabashi if they understand the ongoing conflict between postcolonialist* scholars (scholars inquiring into the various cultural and social legacies of colonialism) and the institutions and organizations mentioned above. Dabashi views these as belittling Iran's cultural history while helping to perpetuate an American brand of imperialism.

NOTES

1   Hamid Dabashi, *Iran: A People Interrupted* (New York: The New Press, 2007), xii.

2   See John J. Mearsheimer and Stephen Walt, *The Israel Lobby and U.S. Foreign Policy* (New York: Farrar, Straus and Giroux, 2007).

3   Dabashi, *A People Interrupted*, 7.

4   See Kenneth Pollack, *Arabs at War: Military Effectiveness, 1948–1991* (Lincoln: University of Nebraska Press, 2004); and *A Path Out of the Desert: A Grand Strategy for America in the Middle East* (New York: Random House, 2009).

5   Kenneth Pollack, *The Threatening Storm: The Case for Invading Iraq* (New York: Random House, 2002).

6   Kenneth Pollack, *The Persian Puzzle: The Conflict between Iran and America* (New York: Random House, 2005).

7   Pollack, *The Persian Puzzle*, 375–6.

8   Azar Nafisi, *Reading Lolita in Tehran: A Memoir in Books* (New York: Random House, 2003).

9   For example, Paul Allen, "Review: Reading Lolita in Tehran: A Story of Love, Books and Revolution by Azar Nafisi," *Guardian,* September 12, 2003.

10 Hamid Dabashi, "Native Informers and the Making of the American Empire," *Al-Ahram Weekly*, June 1, 2006, accessed September 10, 2015, http://www.campus-watch.org/article/id/2802.

11 Dabashi, *A People Interrupted*, 11.

MODULE 4
THE AUTHOR'S CONTRIBUTION

KEY POINTS

- Hamid Dabashi set out to defend Iranian history and ideas against Western misinterpretation at a time of hostility following the 2001 terrorist attacks on New York and the US-led invasion of Iraq in 2003.

- *Iran: A People Interrupted* is a major contribution to scholarship because it explains why Iran is so resistant to outside influence.

- Though Dabashi's methodology draws heavily from postcolonial studies,* his study of the literary evolution of Iranian thought is entirely original.

Author's Aims

Hamid Dabashi's objective when writing *Iran: A People Interrupted* was to challenge the "clichéd categorization of Iran as a country caught between a belligerent tradition* and an alien modernity,* and to adopt a more historically nuanced, culturally multifaceted, and materially grounded reading of Iran."[1]

Building on the groundbreaking work of the influential postcolonial scholar Edward Said,* Dabashi set out to take on "orientalists"* (such as the British American historian and public intellectual Bernard Lewis)* for falsely asserting there is "a great insurmountable divide between Islam and the West" while promising to "offer a more balanced reading of Iran and its discontents."[2] He says there is no "binary opposition" between "tradition" and "modernity," which are artificial constructions.

As an Iranian, a Muslim, and a New Yorker, Dabashi was deeply affected by the 9/11* terrorist attacks on the United States in 2001. In

> ❝ *Iran: A People Interrupted* is an important book because it succeeds in creating a sensibility that harbors no apologia for the Islamic Republic while avoiding the incentive to posit Iran in the shadows of a neoliberal utopia … His book anticipates the kind of cultural and political possibilities that will arise as the world sees a decentering of American hegemony and Iran opens up to other nations. ❞
>
> Kouross Esmaeli, "*Iran: A People Interrupted* (Review)"

particular, he was concerned with the way in which Bush administration* officials sought to reshape the Middle East, starting first with the US-led invasion of Iraq.* Not long after 9/11 it also became clear that the Bush administration had Iran in its sight as well. In 2002, President George W. Bush* famously accused the Islamic Republic* of being part of an "axis of evil"* that supported terrorism and was trying to develop nuclear weapons.* Dabashi felt obliged to defend the place of his birth.

Dabashi is a professor of literature, not foreign affairs, so he tackled orientalist myths by examining Iran's history through the work of its writers and thinkers.

Approach
Dabashi chose an unusual method for exposing the patronizing attitudes towards Iran in Western literature and media. He did not systematically refute "orientalist"* scholarship by comparing and contrasting Western and Iranian texts. Instead, *Interrupted* uses Iranian literature, poetry, cinema, personal stories, and political commentary to reveal the nation's struggle against foreign imperialism* (from Britain, Russia, and the United States) and oppression at home (from the monarchy and religious leaders.)

The intellectual framework of *Interrupted* reflects the author's heritage and literary prowess along with his academic environment. Dabashi is an influential voice in both popular and academic discussion surrounding decolonization* (the period between 1946 and 1975 when European imperial powers granted independence to their colonial lands), modernity, and contemporary Iranian politics. His mission in *Interrupted* is to bring his adopted country (America) to a greater understanding of the rich intellectual heritage of his homeland (Iran).

Dabashi works his way chronologically through 200 years of literature, poetry, and politics in Iran, showing how they overlap and evolve. This intellectual and political development is presented not as a product of wholesale acceptance of imported Western political ideals, but rather as a response to them. This, in turn, is Dabashi's key to the Islamic Republic's intense anti-colonial* ideology and hostility towards Americans, seen by most Iranians as modern-day imperialists.*

Contribution in Context

Although Dabashi draws heavily from the postcolonialist school of thought, *Interrupted* is an entirely original study. The strength of Dabashi's text springs from his comprehensive knowledge of Iranian history, politics, and literature. There is no other scholar in the English-speaking world more familiar with Iranian literature than Dabashi.

This gives him the necessary expertise to apply Edward Said's method of literary criticism to intellectual developments inside Iran and to political events. Though Dabashi owes his intellectual framework to Said, he presents Iran as a successful case study in support of his mentor's theory that Western scholars present a warped view of non-Western history.

Interrupted differs significantly from typical English-language studies of Iran. Most, such as the diplomat and academic Michael Axworthy's* *Revolutionary Iran,*[3] focus on the uprising and its aftermath. Or they investigate the lives of key figures, as the Iranian

American historian Abbas Milani* does in his book *The Shah*.[4] Although both works are valuable studies of Iran, neither author set out to explore and explain Iran's literary evolution. This is because Axworthy and Milani are scholars of politics or history, unlike Dabashi who is a scholar of postmodernism. Therefore although all three fall within the same broad discipline by writing on Iran, *Interrupted* stands alone in both its content and the nature of its argument.

NOTES

1   Hamid Dabashi, *Iran: A People Interrupted* (New York: The New Press, 2007), 10.

2   Dabashi, *A People Interrupted*, 10.

3   Michael Axworthy, *Revolutionary Iran: A History of the Islamic Republic* (New York: Penguin, 2013).

4   Abbas Milani, *The Shah* (New York: Palgrave Macmillan, 2012).

SECTION 2
IDEAS

MODULE 5
MAIN IDEAS

KEY POINTS

- The widespread Western theory of an Iran caught between "tradition"* and "modernity"* is wrong, argues Hamid Dabashi, who uses the history of literature to show how Iranians developed an ideology of resistance.

- This "anti-colonial modernity" evolved naturally over the generations through interaction between Iranian intellectuals, who also engaged with ideals, such as the form of protest known as civil disobedience,* that arose from the Enlightenment* to cope with oppression from home and abroad.

- *Iran: A People Interrupted* demonstrates this original interpretation of Iranian history with a journey through 200 years of Iran's intellectual and artistic development.

Key Themes

Hamid Dabashi has two clear messages in *Iran: A People Interrupted*. The first is that Iranian people developed a national ideology of resistance because they faced suppression from either foreign powers, or royal or religious Iranian rulers. He also speaks out against the simplistic, age-old "orientalist"* description of Iran as caught in an endless battle between tradition and modernity.

Interrupted analyzes the relationship between Iran's intellectual and political elite over the course of the last 200 years. Dabashi presents this interaction as the natural evolution of an anti-colonial* ideology of resistance. It springs from the contradiction at the heart of colonial modernity—domineering nations claim to bring progressive ideas but impose them by force. The Enlightenment era of the seventeenth and

> ❝ Writing history is resisting power, particularly when eradicating history and cultivating a deliberate amnesia, in theory and practice, is the single most abiding manner of projecting the open-ended power of this [American] empire and discrediting the necessary modes of contesting and resisting it. ❞
>
> Hamid Dabashi, *Iran: A People Interrupted*

eighteenth centuries championed reason and liberty over tradition. It promised people in the developing world freedom at exactly the time they were being colonized and exploited by Western powers. Iran was never a colony but was under constant pressure from intrusive colonial powers. This bred an alternative position in Iran—modernity that was modern in the Enlightenment sense but rooted in anti-colonial resistance.

Interrupted is essentially a review of the literature that Dabashi knows so well. He uses the stories and ideas of poets, thinkers, and politicians to trace Iran's intellectual evolution. But it is also a passionate critique of major political and academic assumptions about Iran. Dabashi draws on philosophy, art, literature, and his own life to question the legacy of imperialism,*the pervasive power of orientalism,* and the caricature of Iran as caught between tradition and modernity. Dabashi severely criticizes the scholars he believes portray Iran in a misguided and essentially racist fashion.

Exploring the Ideas

Dabashi argues that the colonial definition of modern was a "self-raising/other-lowering project … to benefit a small fraction of the world's population," mostly in Europe, while disenfranchising "the overwhelming majority of humanity" elsewhere.[1] Modernity was thrust upon the rest of the world down the barrel of a gun, making it just another element of colonialism.*

This was not to say that Iranians did not appreciate the philosophical progress the Enlightenment brought. Dabashi observes that anti-colonial modernity was "not *reactive* against the philosophical articulation of modernity in the course of European Enlightenment … but entirely *proactive* and rooted in the anticolonial struggles of peoples around the globe."[2]

It was simply a new reality, based on the struggle of indigenous people against their colonial masters. Although Iran was never a formal colony, its anti-colonial outlook grew out of its relationship with the West, mainly the imperial powers of Britain and Russia and later the United States. Iran was often subject to colonial interference and intervention, including the 1941 invasion by Britain and Russia who overthrew the head of state, Reza Pahlavi, and replaced him with his son, Mohammad Reza Pahlavi.*

A major element of *Interrupted* is Dabashi's loathing of orientalist academics. Using Edward Said's* concept of orientalism (roughly, the idea that the West is superior to other cultures), Dabashi attacks the work of "mercenary" Western scholars, including the expert on Middle Eastern affairs Kenneth Pollack* and the historian Bernard Lewis.* He accuses them of contriving to "authenticate and corroborate the principality of a European modernity that at its core was racist and essentialist, and as such excluded … the vast majority of the world."[3] Dabashi accuses Pollack of helping "pave the way for the illegal and immoral US-led invasion of Iraq and the subsequent murder of tens of thousands of innocent people,"[4] in his book *The Threatening Storm: The Case for Invading Iraq.*[5] Dabashi also takes aim at Iranian scholars, including Azar Nafisi.* He accuses Nafisi of "deliberate amnesia"[6] and of accepting lucrative contracts to "reduce their own nation to 'security issues' for the US empire." He rejects the debate these scholars have created over whether Iran is traditional or modern because he argues it is neither.[7]

Dabashi attempts to put a different image of Iran before the world:

one that stands apart from "the ever-tightening confines of the political and ideological polarization between the Islamic Republic* [of Iran] and the American project to redefine the Middle East in its own image."[8]

Language and Expression

The ideas in *Interrupted* can be difficult to decipher because of Dabashi's tendency to use philosophical language and complex sentence structure. To fully understand the text, it helps to have some knowledge of philosophy, Iranian history, and the intellectual debate surrounding decolonization* (a process, with political and cultural implications, which begins when a colonial power gives up its possessions). Dabashi presumes his readers have a working knowledge of these areas.

Dabashi makes his argument by organizing *Interrupted* along chronological lines. There are seven chapters, each dealing with a separate phase of Iran's intellectual development over the last 200 years. He opens, though, with a scathing critique of leading scholars of foreign relations and international relations theory, including the international relations scholar Samuel Huntington* and the political scientist Francis Fukuyama,* and "orientalists" such as Pollack and Lewis. He accuses them all of being "dead wrong" in their approach to history. Dabashi promises to write "people back into the history of their regional and global resistance."[9]

He begins his journey through Iran's rich intellectual heritage with the renowned thirteenth-century Persian poet Sa'di,* whose themes included justice and liberty.* Sa'di's writing influenced Enlightenment intellectuals such as the French essayist Voltaire* and the German playwright and poet Johann Wolfgang von Goethe.* It was also read by Benjamin Franklin,* one of the Founding Fathers of the United States. Sa'di also influenced the American philosopher Henry David Thoreau,* who developed the concept of civil disobedience—a form of protest in which specific laws are deliberately flouted because they are seen as unjust. Dabashi argues that in this way the natural Iranian inclination to oppose domination and oppression had influenced the European intellectual tradition.

Dabashi moves on to the first tentative contacts between Iran and the West in the early 1800s, which led to developments such as the simplification of Persian prose.* The problem, as Dabashi observes, was not with the message of the Enlightenment but the way it was conveyed "through the gun barrel of colonialism."[10] To highlight the negative impact of colonial pressure Dabashi examines four periods of modern Iranian history. These are the Constitutional Revolution (1905–11),* in which the Iranian people demanded government reform; the Pahlavi dynasty* (1925–79); the Iranian Revolution* (1978–9), an uprising that saw the ruling Pahlavi family overthrown; and the Islamic Republic* (1980 to the present). In each case, he shows how the Iranian people's fierce resistance to internal and external subjugation developed into deep-seated anti-colonial sentiment.

NOTES

1 Hamid Dabashi, *Iran: A People Interrupted* (New York: The New Press, 2007), 250.

2 Dabashi, *A People Interrupted*, 251.

3 Dabashi, *A People Interrupted*, 250.

4 Dabashi, *A People Interrupted*, 7.

5 Kenneth Pollack, *The Threatening Storm: The Case for Invading Iraq* (New York: Random House, 2002).

6 Dabashi, *A People Interrupted*, 7–8.

7 Dabashi, *A People Interrupted*, 250.

8   Kouross Esmaeli, review of *Iran: A People Interrupted*, by Hamid Dabashi, *Comparative Studies of South Asia, Africa and the Middle East* 28, no. 2 (2008): 375.

9   Dabashi, *A People Interrupted*, 9.

10   Dabashi, *A People Interrupted*, 46.

MODULE 6
SECONDARY IDEAS

KEY POINTS

- *Iran: A People Interrupted* explores how developments in the world of ideas affected political events.

- Hamid Dabashi shows how Iranian writers played a key role in challenging the political elite and bringing about major reforms.

- The very subject of the book—Iranian literature—is often ignored as critics focus on the personal elements of the book, including Dabashi's forthright opinions about other academics.

Other Ideas

Hamid Dabashi makes a powerful argument for a new understanding of Iran away from patronizing "orientalist"* studies. His criticism of fellow scholars and contribution to the public debate over relations between the Middle East and America has taken attention away from other elements of *Iran: A People Interrupted*.

Dabashi's examination of Iran's rich intellectual history and the links he makes with political developments in Iran receive much less attention than his more controversial opinions. These secondary themes, however, are important to Dabashi's main argument—that Iranian ideology evolved over 200 years through the interaction of thinkers and politicians in Iran, including an exchange of ideas with Europe.

Interrupted is a journey through Iran's rich intellectual heritage, starting with the renowned Persian poet Sa'di.* His ideas had a major influence on key Enlightenment* intellectuals, including the American statesman Benjamin Franklin,* the first North American to read his work. Dabashi then examines how contact between Iran and the West

> ❝ The single most definitive fact of our lives over the last two hundred years has been our consistent battle with the colonial and imperial domination of our destiny—a domination facilitated too eagerly by its local beneficiaries. ❞
>
> Hamid Dabashi, *Iran: A People Interrupted*

influenced important Iranian thinkers and affected major political developments inside Iran. In particular, the simplification of Persian, the introduction of newspapers, and exposure to Western parliamentary democracy* had a significant impact on Iranian history, culture, and politics and helped mold its national ideology of resistance to internal and external subjugation.

Exploring the Ideas

Dabashi's review of Iranian literature begins with a discussion of how Persian poetry influenced leading Enlightenment intellectuals in the seventeenth and eighteenth centuries. Dabashi writes that "no one would believe that the first person on this continent to have read … the legendary Persian poet [Sa'di] was none other than a gentleman statesman, printer, inventor, publisher, fan of flying kites, and man of letters from Philadelphia … Mr. Benjamin Franklin himself!"[1]

He then examines the historical relationship between Iranian and Western ideas. The early eighteenth century saw young Iranians visiting Europe and encountering representative government and a literate population. Among them was Mirza Saleh Shirazi,* a man who both simplified Persian prose so ordinary people could learn to read, and started the first Iranian newspaper.

Such changes transformed Iran into a modern society built on a growing intellectual elite. This educated class pressed for political change, culminating in the assassination of Shah (king) Nasir al-Din

Shah Qajar* in 1896. Then the Constitutional Revolution* of 1905–11 brought in a constitutional monarchy.

Dabashi's writing focuses on Iranian intellectuals and writers about whom few in the West have much knowledge. *Interrupted* is packed with information new to Western scholars. It also explains the role of the branch of the Islamic religion known as Shi'ist* Islam in the Iranian psyche. As a minority sect in Islam it was always a religion of protest. It dates back to the Battle of Karbala* when Imam Husayn (grandson of the Prophet Muhammad)* refused to recognize the prophet's successor Yazid and was killed in an act of martyrdom. Shi'ism is the dominant religion in Iran and Dabashi argues that Shi'a traditions of resistance and protest can be seen in the modern mindset. This is a very important contribution to the study of Iran's political actions today.

Overlooked

The element of *Interrupted* that has been most overlooked is actually the very foundation of the book—Iranian literature. Most of the attention Hamid Dabashi received for his text centered on his personal attacks on academic enemies. Not enough consideration is given to the actual substance of Dabashi's contribution to the Western understanding of Iran's literature and intellectual roots. This valuable contribution to the study of Iran's ideology of resistance deserves a wider readership.

The complexity of Dabashi's arguments and prose has contributed to *Interrupted* being overlooked. Another factor is his outright rejection of the work of influential international relations theorists such as Samuel Huntington* (noted for his 1996 book *The Clash of Civilizations and the Remaking of World Order*).

For all these reasons many scholars of Iranian foreign policy or regional security issues have neglected *Interrupted*. This is regrettable because Dabashi's explanation of Iran's intellectual and ideological foundations could benefit Western foreign-policy experts seeking to engage the Iranians in dialogue and help them better frame their diplomatic strategy.

NOTES

1 Hamid Dabashi, *Iran: A People Interrupted* (New York: The New Press, 2007), 14–15.

MODULE 7
ACHIEVEMENT

KEY POINTS

- *Iran: A People Interrupted* tells the dramatic story of how Iran's intellectual history was bound up with political developments in order to forge a national ideology of resistance.

- Hamid Dabashi's groundbreaking study was published when Iran dominated international headlines, making it a timely contribution to public debate.

- Unfortunately Dabashi's achievement was overshadowed by the angry reaction to his uncompromising criticism of fellow scholars and commentators.

Assessing the Argument

Hamid Dabashi's main reason for writing *Iran: A People Interrupted* was to challenge the categorization—prevalent among Western readers—of Iran as a country caught between tradition* and modernity.*[1] Certainly Dabashi's plan was ambitious. It also involved drawing Iran's artistic journey together with his own life story and opinions. In this way he set out to prove Iran's national psyche is a result of centuries of struggle against colonial* imperialism* from Britain, Russia, and the United States, and internal suppression from kings and religious leaders.

Dabashi achieves his objective by piecing together Iran's intellectual evolution along a carefully plotted timeline. He starts with the influential poet Sa'di,* moves on to the Constitutional Revolution,* charts the rise and fall of the Pahlavi royal family,* then explains the Iranian Revolution* and the rise of the Islamic Republic of Iran.* Dabashi looks closely at the key writers in each phase and explains how their writing affected Iranian politics. His knowledge of Iranian

> ❝ Dabashi brilliantly demonstrates that it was 'the contemporaneity of current concerns' that motivated all of the Islamic ideologues as they reacted to the 'immediacies of contemporary Muslim realities.' At a level of detail found in no other book, he shows how these ideologues reconstructed both the 'Islamic' and the 'Ideology,' concluding that the 'Islamic' was reconstructed 'from the medieval memory of its past remembrance, under which the most varied forms of secular ("Western") claims to political salvation are to be propagated.' ❞
>
> Reza Afshari, "A Critique of Dabashi's Reconstruction of Islamic Ideology as a Prerequisite for the Iranian Revolution"

history, politics, and literature is so extensive that *Interrupted* amounts to a convincing case for Iran's intellectual development being unique. This makes Dabashi's work an impressive feat of scholarship.

Achievement in Context

The timing of *Interrupted* was perfect. When Dabashi's book was published in 2007, Iran was at the forefront of international politics due to its controversial nuclear program* and outspoken president Mahmoud Ahmadinejad.* The world was deeply divided over how to respond to reports about the rapid expansion of Iran's nuclear enrichment program. The Bush* administration, concerned that Iran was trying to create nuclear weapons, convinced the United Nations Security Council to adopt sanctions in an attempt to force the Iranians back to the negotiating table.[2]

Ahmadinejad's antagonistic approach to foreign relations did not help the situation. In addition to the rapid expansion of Iran's nuclear capability, Ahmadinejad's anti-Semitic* rhetoric about Israel—that is, his openly anti-Jewish sentiment—escalated tensions further. The disputed presidential elections in 2009* saw him secure a second term, which was no better than the first. Throughout 2011 his outspoken approach increased the likelihood of an Israeli or American attack on its nuclear facilities.

However, the surprise election of the cleric Hassan Rouhani* as president in 2013 and an unexpected thaw in US–Iran relations led to the signing of a comprehensive nuclear agreement in July 2015, in which Iran agreed to scale back its nuclear enrichment program for at least 15 years and allow intensive inspections in exchange for sanctions relief. These developments make *Interrupted* all the more relevant to the policymakers and diplomats engaged in negotiations who seek a better understanding of Iran.

Limitations

In many ways Dabashi's book is very rooted in its time. Regular references to contemporary events such as the 2001 terrorist attacks on America (9/11)* and other books written in the same decade certainly date the text. Even so, *Interrupted* remains a brilliant exposition of Iran's intellectual history that, in itself, is timeless.

The major limiting factors of *Interrupted* include Dabashi's highly complex language, which seems aimed at the academic literary world rather than a broad readership. He also has a tendency to go off at tangents that are not absolutely crucial to his argument, and makes open attacks on many leading foreign-policy scholars.

Dabashi's use of highly philosophical language, convoluted argument, and complex prose appears to have limited the number of people who can grasp the work's conceptual framework or overall goal. As one critic observed, "the language of the book can at times wax very academic, employing words, phrases, and concepts that will make [his] arguments harder to understand for many readers."[3] There are also difficulties with Dabashi's style. Though *Interrupted* is presented chronologically, he often jumps back and forth between discussing ancient Iranian poetry and contemporary politics, again making understanding his arguments more challenging.

NOTES

1   Hamid Dabashi, *Iran: A People Interrupted* (New York: The New Press, 2007), 10.

2   Elissa Gootman, "Security Council Approves Sanctions Against Iran Over Nuclear Program," *New York Times*, December 24, 2006.

3   Keith Rosenthal, "Correcting Western Views of Iran," review of *Iran: A People Interrupted*, by Hamid Dabashi, *International Socialist Review* 55 (2007).

MODULE 8
PLACE IN THE AUTHOR'S WORK

KEY POINTS

- Although Hamid Dabashi's career is largely devoted to studying the philosophy behind the politics of resistance, he also writes on Iranian art and film.

- *Iran: A People Interrupted* was the product of Dabashi's decades-long scholarly interest in Iranian intellectual history, art, poetry, and philosophy.

- The text was only moderately successful in comparison to Dabashi's other works and more famous studies of postcolonialism.*

Positioning

Hamid Dabashi began studying at the University of Tehran in August 1970, at the height of Shah (king) Mohammad Reza Pahlavi's* rule. The young Dabashi was already a social activist who read banned books despite the threat of being caught by SAVAK,* the Shah's secret police.

Dabashi speaks openly of his childhood in *Iran: A People Interrupted*. He shares many personal stories about growing up during the reign of the Shah and his experiences in the aftermath of the Iranian Revolution* of 1978–9. This era saw Dabashi's democratic aspirations for Iran destroyed by the new religious leaders and had a profound effect on the ideas in *Interrupted*.

Dabashi published his first book, *Authority in Islam*, in 1989. Setting the stage for his career, he used the German sociologist Max Weber's* concept of charismatic authority* to analyze the social and cultural responses of three branches of Islam (Sunni,* Shi'a,* and Khariji)* to the transformation of the Prophet Muhammad's* authority and the prophetic movement.[1] Most of Dabashi's earlier work focuses on the

> **❝** Hamid Dabashi is one of the foremost exponents today of postcolonial critical theory, whose work deserves to be called post-colonial with all the multivalence of this description. In his work, post-coloniality does not mean a denial or denunciation of the modern European tradition of philosophy and social theory, but their effortless absorption into a larger, more complex reflection. **❞**
>
> Sudipta Kaviraj, "The World is My Home"

relationship between philosophy, literature, and the politics of resistance—often using Iran as a case study.[2] Therefore, by the time he wrote *Interrupted*, Dabashi was an established scholar.

Integration

Dabashi's writing can be divided into two categories. The most important of these, which includes *Interrupted*, deals with the politics of resistance and often uses Iran to argue the case. His other works focus on art and film.

Dabashi's political studies include contributions to Seyyed Hossein and Oliver Leaman's *History of Islamic Philosophy* (1996); *Truth and Narrative: The Untimely Thoughts of 'Ayn al-Qudat* (1999); *Staging a Revolution: The Art of Persuasion in the Islamic Republic of Iran* (2001); and *Theology of Discontent: The Ideological Foundation of the Islamic Revolution in Iran* (1993, 2005).[3] *Interrupted* was a result of Dabashi's deep interest in Iran's intellectual development but also written out of a desire to explain his complex country to the West.

Interrupted set the stage for his later work on understanding the Middle East. This includes *Post Orientalism: Knowledge and Power in Time of Terror* (2008),[4] an analysis of ideas first introduced in *Interrupted*. Dabashi's interest in decolonization* and resistance are evident in

Islamic Liberation Theology: Resisting the Empire (2008); *Iran, The Green Movement* and the USA: The Fox and the Paradox* (2010); *Shi'ism: A Religion of Protest* (2011); *The Arab Spring:* The End of Postcolonialism* (2012); and *Corpus Anarchicum: Political Protest, Suicidal Violence, and the Making of the Posthuman Body* (2012).[5]

Dabashi's other area of intellectual interest is Iranian art and cinema. His books on these include *Close Up: Iranian Cinema, Past, Present and Future* (2001) and *Masters and Masterpieces of Iranian Cinema* (2007).[6] He sits on the juries of a number of international film festivals and advises several major producers.[7]

As an Iranian-born American, Dabashi has witnessed Iran go from one form of tyranny to another and then observed the Bush administration* threaten his country with war. So there is no question that the work was shaped by personal experience and historical context. *Interrupted* is a natural development of the author's earlier work and a comfortable stepping-stone for his subsequent publications.

Significance

According to Google Scholar, *Interrupted* has been cited in at least 94 different publications around the world. This is a significant number. But his *Theology of Discontent: The Ideological Foundation of the Islamic Revolution in Iran* has been cited more than 250 times, making it his most popular text. Meanwhile *The Arab Spring: The End of Postcolonialism* has been cited 131 times, and his *Close Up: Iranian Cinema, Past, Present and Future*, 114 times. This shows that while *Interrupted* is considered significant and referred to often by fellow scholars, it is not among his top three most cited publications.

Although *Interrupted* fits comfortably in the field of postcolonial studies, it has not become one of its leading texts. Fellow scholars in the field are cited far more often than Dabashi. For example, the Martinique-born philosopher Frantz Fanon's* classic *The Wretched of the Earth* has been cited more than 10,000 times, Jean-Paul Sartre's*

Being and Nothingness more than 7,000, and Edward Said's* *Orientalism* more than 1,500—but it is unfair to expect any modern text to be as popular as the scholarship that established a field of study. The very purpose of subsequent scholarship is to support, modify, or refute previous work. To this end, Dabashi was entirely successful in applying the model established in Fanon, Sartre, and Said's work to Iran. At the same time, Dabashi introduced a fascinating new element—the question of whether literature and art can influence politics.

NOTES

1   Hamid Dabashi, *Authority in Islam: From the Rise of Muhammad to the Establishment of the Umayyads* (New Brunswick, NJ: Transaction Publishers, 1989).

2   Hamid Dabashi, contributions to *History of Islamic Philosophy*, ed. Seyyed Hossein Nasr and Oliver Leaman (London: Routledge, 1996); *Truth and Narrative: The Untimely Thoughts of 'Ayn al-Qudat al-Hamadhani* (London: Curzon Press, 1999); *Theology of Discontent: The Ideological Foundation of the Islamic Revolution in Iran* (New Brunswick, NJ: Transaction Publishers, 2005); with Peter Chelkowski, *Staging a Revolution: The Art of Persuasion in the Islamic Republic of Iran* (New York: New York University Press, 2002).

3   Dabashi, *History of Islamic Philosophy*; *Truth and Narrative*; *Staging a Revolution*; and *Theology of Discontent*.

4   Dabashi, *Theology of Discontent*.

5   Hamid Dabashi, *Islamic Liberation Theology: Resisting the Empire* (London: Routledge, 2009); *Iran, The Green Movement and the USA: The Fox and the Paradox* (London: Zed Books, 2010); *Shi'ism: A Religion of Protest* (Cambridge, MA: Belknap Press, 2011); *The Arab Spring: The End of Postcolonialism* (London: Zed Books, 2012); and *Corpus Anarchicum: Political Protest, Suicidal Violence, and the Making of the Posthuman Body* (New York: Palgrave MacMillan, 2012).

6   Hamid Dabashi, *Close Up: Iranian Cinema, Past, Present and Future* (New York: Verso, 2001); and *Masters and Masterpieces of Iranian Cinema* (New York: Mage, 2007).

7   For details about Dabashi's involvement in film, see his website: www.HamidDabashi.com/cinema-and-art/.

SECTION 3
IMPACT

MODULE 9
THE FIRST RESPONSES

KEY POINTS

- Criticism of *Iran: A People Interrupted* centered largely on Dabashi's aggressive attacks on scholars and public intellectuals, his alleged arrogance, and his tendency to use highly sophisticated language.

- There is no record of Dabashi responding directly to any of these critiques.

- Ultimately it was Dabashi's attacks on other scholars that proved to be the most important factor shaping the reception of the text.

Criticism

Given the way Hamid Dabashi attacked those he disliked in *Iran: A People Interrupted*, it is not surprising that he received some criticism in return. The vast majority of criticism related to his attacks on other scholars, though it did not come from the targets directly. Referencing Joseph Stalin,* the notoriously brutal leader of the Soviet Union* between the mid-1920s and 1953, the conservative Canadian journalist Robert Fulford* wrote in the Canadian *National Post* newspaper that "Dabashi's frame of reference veers from Stalin to Edward Said,"* accusing him of employing totalitarian methods to "convert culture into politics" and branding everything "he dislikes as an example of imperialism."*[1]

Another writer, the political scientist Kaveh Afrasiabi,* accused Dabashi of being an arrogant "pseudo-intellectual," who adopted an "outright dismissive attitude toward authors he disagrees with." He felt Dabashi's approach was "utterly absurd" and smacked of "self-styled intellectual McCarthyism"*[2]—in other words, he made

> ❝Dabashi's frame of reference veers from Stalin to Edward Said. Like a Stalinist, he tries to convert culture into politics, the first step toward totalitarianism. Like the late Edward Said, he brands every thought he dislikes as an example of imperialism, expressing the West's desire for hegemony over the downtrodden (even when oil-rich) nations of the Third World. ❞
>
> Robert Fulford, *The National Post*

unsupported accusations in order to back up his argument. Afrasiabi believed that Dabashi's caustic approach was a mistake, since "intellectuals cease to be intellectuals once they attempt to pass off overemotional, spurious intellectual persuasion as true enlightenment."[3] Yet another writer, a scholar of the Middle East called John Cappucci,* was equally put off by Dabashi's caustic approach, describing his writing as "excessively opinionated," "pugnacious," "exasperating," and "reading almost like a rant."[4]

Perhaps the greatest criticism leveled at *Interrupted* was of the highly philosophical language and overly complex prose that made Dabashi's ideas difficult to grasp. Indeed, Cappucci is correct when he observes that while Dabashi claims to write a history dedicated to dispelling distorted historical views about Iran, he ultimately "diverged from this straight path and presents his readers with inconsistencies, misconceptions, and unsubstantiated opinions."[5]

However, the book was also welcomed as an alternative to Western interpretations of Iran. The American political commentator Ron Jacobs* commended the work for creating "a new historiography"* (methods of writing about history) on Iran, turning "conventional western scholarship on that country upside down," and standing out as "a cry against the increasing tribalization of world politics by the theocrats and their allies in Washington, Iran, Delhi, Tel Aviv and elsewhere."[6] Jacobs applauded Dabashi for challenging the right-wing political scientist Francis Fukuyama's* claim that liberal democracy* signaled that there was an "end of history," "just because Western policymakers and their sycophantic intellectuals say there is." Indeed, he added, "history remains alive and is being written by the very forces those intellectuals and policymakers disregard and try to subjugate."[7]

Responses

Dabashi has not responded directly to any of the more obvious criticisms of *Interrupted*, such as factual errors, contradictions, complex language, or emotional dismissal of any scholar who disagrees with his point of view. He has not published later editions of the book that address these issues, so no critical dialogue has taken place. This is unfortunate because in recent years he has become known for passionate engagement with his critics.

The author does, however, continue to attack people he deems to be "orientalist"* scholars, including leading historians Bernard Lewis* and Abbas Milani* who have a very different view of Iran. In an interview with Aslan Media in 2012, Dabashi attacked Lewis for continuing to perpetuate orientalist views of the Middle East: "All we need is just to imagine the face of Bernard Lewis and we have such a visceral revulsion that we become paralyzed ... As I have long since argued, we need to change the interlocutors. These Orientalists are no longer worth our attention. History, our people, people at large, have left them behind and so must we."[8] The problem with such personal attacks is that they obscure the more substantial differences these scholars might have about Iran and its people.

Conflict and Consensus

It is difficult to assess the impact of Dabashi's study on the larger political and academic debate about Iran because *Interrupted* only appeared in 2007. The books he has written since have been more popular with readers, so it seems unlikely that *Interrupted* will suddenly emerge as a leading text on the subject. The main obstacle to Dabashi's book achieving a better academic reputation is the number of open attacks on individuals. The book's appeal is also hampered by the complex language Dabashi employs to convey his ideas. If Dabashi returned to the book to tackle these aspects it could emerge as one of the best texts on Iranian history. Unfortunately, this seems unlikely.

There is no question that *Interrupted* is an impressive contribution to the study of Iranian history, intellectual life, and politics. But there is no evidence to suggest it has substantially influenced the debates surrounding the scholarship of modern Iran. It has not had an impact on the conflict between neoconservative* and liberal positions over how to respond to Iran's nuclear program.* This is despite the significant improvement in US–Iran relations since 2013, culminating in the signing of a nuclear agreement in 2015. Nevertheless, to scholars of Iranian history, politics, and literature, there is no doubt that *Interrupted* is a very important contribution to our understanding of the historical roots of current events.

NOTES

1 Robert Fulford, "Reading Lolita at Columbia," *National Post*, November 6, 2006.

2 Kaveh Afrasiabi, "Pseudo-intellectualism on Iran: Review: *Iran: A People Interrupted*, by Hamid Dabashi," *Asia Times*, November 15, 2008.

3 Afrasiabi, "Pseudo-intellectualism on Iran."

4 John Cappucci, review of *Iran: A People Interrupted*, by Hamid Dabashi, *International Journal of Middle Eastern Studies* 41, no. 3 (2009): 488.

5 Cappucci, review of *Iran: A People Interrupted*, 489.

6   Ron Jacobs, "Transcending the Colonizer's History," review of *Iran: A People Interrupted*, by Hamid Dabashi, *OpEd News*, January 1, 2008.

7   Jacobs, "Transcending the Colonizer's History."

8   *Aslan Media*, "On Representation: Dr. Hamid Dabashi on the Exiled Intellectual as Cultural Artist," November 15, 2012, accessed June 8, 2015, http://aslanmedia.com/arts-culture/mideast-culture/20676–on-representation-dr-hamid-dabashi-on-the-exiled-intellectual-as-cultural-artist#sthash.9UAJoetd.dpuf.

MODULE 10
THE EVOLVING DEBATE

KEY POINTS

- Assessing the long-term impact of *Iran: A People Interrupted* is difficult because it was only published in 2007.

- While no distinct school of thought has emerged around Hamid Dabashi's book, it has helped to revive interest in postcolonial studies.*

- Though Dabashi makes an important contribution to understanding Iran's intellectual history and national psyche, Edward Said* remains the most influential scholar in the field.

Uses and Problems

Since Hamid Dabashi's *Iran: A People Interrupted* appeared in 2007 Iran has remained at the forefront of international politics. Events include Iran's controversial nuclear program,* the violence after the disputed presidential elections in 2009,* a heightened threat of an Israeli or an American attack in 2011, the surprise election of the cleric Hassan Rouhani* in 2012, the unexpected return to the negotiating table with the US in 2013–15, and the signing of a nuclear agreement in July 2015. These events make *Interrupted* relevant to scholars and politicians seeking to understand Iran.

Although it is too early to judge whether *Interrupted* has influenced the circles in which foreign policy is decided, Dabashi continues to fuel the intellectual debate. He followed the book with a succession of hard–hitting publications. These tackle the issues of US foreign policy, imperialism,* and decolonization,* and again champion the politics of resistance. *Islamic Liberation Theology: Resisting the Empire*[1] analyzes the Islamic ideology of the Iranian Revolution.* However, one critic

> ❝Hamid Dabashi's writings on Iranian culture and politics brilliantly re-imagine the rich heritage of a shared past and a conflicted present. His reflections on revolution and nationhood, poetry and cinema, philosophy and the sacred, are urgent, provocative, complex, and highly original. ❞
>
> Timothy Mitchell, "The World is My Home"

described this as "little more than a rehash of Iranian religio-political literature" present in *Interrupted*.[2] In his edited volume, *The Green Movement* in Iran*,[3] Dabashi was criticized for failing to actually explain the movement or its goals very clearly. Many of the problems evident in *Interrupted* are present in this book, such as taking potshots at authors he dislikes, decrying Israel as "a racist apartheid* state," and as one critic pointed out, being "unable to escape the jargon of academic theory to communicate a point."[4]

Because of these fundamental problems with his work, many scholars have been unwilling to engage him in an open debate. One commentator observed that Dabashi "spectacularly illustrates why few outside the academy take Iranian studies professors seriously."[5] This is one explanation for why *Interrupted* and most of Dabashi's subsequent works have failed to fuel a wider intellectual debate.

Schools of Thought

Although no new school of thought has emerged from *Interrupted*, it makes a valuable contribution to the one established by Edward Said, the leading theorist of postcolonialism. Dabashi, along with thinkers such as Gayatri Chakravorty Spivak,* and Dipesh Chakrabarty,* have contributed to a revival in the field of postcolonial studies. A testament to this growing interest is the founding of the UK-based Postcolonial Studies Association* (PSA). The PSA encourages and helps to finance research, sharing its work at annual conferences. With more than 100 members, the organization proves there is a growing interest in this field of study.

Dabashi has continued to write on postcolonialism and develop many of the ideas he introduced in *Interrupted*. In *Post-Orientalism: Knowledge and Power in Time of Terror*,[6] Dabashi addresses the US-led War on Terror* following the 9/11* terrorist attacks on New York and Washington in 2001. *Islamic Liberation Theology: Resisting the Empire*[7] looks at the politics of resistance in terms of the Islamic forces of Iran's revolution.* In *The Arab Spring:* The End of Postcolonialism*,[8] Dabashi argues that the popular uprisings in the Middle East marked the end of colonial and postcolonial identities. For him, the protests gave rise to new ideologies that abandon nationalism,* socialism,* and Islamism.* Dabashi's continued focus on postcolonial issues demonstrate that he is deeply engaged in this field.

In Current Scholarship

The theoretical approach in *Interrupted* is steeped in the work of Dabashi's colleague and friend Edward Said, who died four years before the book came out. Said's groundbreaking *Orientalism* continues to be an influential text in Dabashi's academic field, especially for those dealing with the Middle East.

Thinkers and commentators who praise Dabashi's work, such as the American historian Rashid Khalidi,* also identify closely with Said. They share a deep commitment to studying the effects of imperialism and the politics of resistance.

With the death of Said in 2003, postcolonial studies broadened beyond his particular concerns, particularly in the United Kingdom. Here the PSA encourages young academics into the field. Despite this, there is no evidence of anyone taking on or adapting Dabashi's highly intellectual, theoretical framework, whereas the PSA's website lists a half-dozen members who cite Said as an influence or his work as an analytical model.[9]

This all suggests that Dabashi's significance comes more from the way he engages in public debates on topical issues in the media. While *Interrupted* is a spectacular study of Iran's literary history, rich with detail and information about the creation of the intellectual and political elite, it will never have the same sweeping influence over scholarship as Said's *Orientalism*.

NOTES

1   Hamid Dabashi, *Islamic Liberation Theology: Resisting the Empire* (London: Routledge, 2009).

2   Stephen Schwartz, review of *Islamic Liberation Theology*, by Hamid Dabashi, *Middle East Quarterly* 16, no. 1 (2009): 84.

3   Hamid Dabashi, *The Green Movement in Iran* (New Brunswick, NJ: Transaction Publishers, 2011).

4   Michael Rubin, review of *The Green Movement in Iran*, by Hamid Dabashi, *Middle East Quarterly* 19, no. 3 (2012): 90.

5   Rubin, review of *The Green Movement*, 90.

6   Hamid Dabashi, *Post-Orientalism: Knowledge and Power in Time of Terror* (New Brunswick, NJ: Transaction Publishers, 2008).

7   Dabashi, *Islamic Liberation Theology*.

8   Hamid Dabashi, *The Arab Spring: The End of Postcolonialism* (London: Zed Books, 2012).

9   "Members," PSA, accessed June 18, 2014, http://www.postcolonialstudiesassociation.co.uk/members/.

MODULE 11
IMPACT AND INFLUENCE TODAY

KEY POINTS

- The status of *Iran: A People Interrupted* has been overshadowed by Hamid Dabashi's more successful works dealing with contemporary issues such as the political uprisings of the Arab Spring*—the protests and civil wars that swept much of the Arab world in 2010.

- The text remains an excellent source of information for scholars and diplomats who want to know why Iran acts the way it does.

- Dabashi's ideas have been useful in the debate over Iran's nuclear program,* which pits neoconservatives* (who advocate military intervention) against liberals (who defend diplomacy and engagement).

Position

Iran has been a major player in global affairs since the days of antiquity. The Iranian Revolution* of 1978–9 drew Iran away from the West and established an Islamic, fiercely anti-American ideology. Today the Iranian government plays a critical role in shaping the politics of the Middle East due to its influence with the region's Shi'a* population. This volatile role on the world stage means that Hamid Dabashi's *Iran: A People Interrupted* will remain a useful text for understanding the political psyche of the Iranian people.

Since the early 1990s, Western powers (particularly the United States and Britain) and their regional allies (especially Saudi Arabia and Israel) have been concerned about Iran's nuclear program. They suspect Iran is trying to build a nuclear bomb. Efforts to resolve the matter in the mid-2000s failed. The situation deteriorated following

> 66 Underneath this current of resistance is a phenomenon forced upon the world by Washington and directly related to how it wants the world to see history. Dabashi denotes this phenomenon as tribalism. It is the logical outcome of the neocon intellectuals and their silent neoliberal cohorts that pretend that history has ended and the West has come out on top. 99
>
> Ron Jacobs, "Review: *Iran: A People Interrupted*"

the 2005 election of Mahmoud Ahmadinejad* to the position of president; he redoubled Iran's enrichment program (a key stage in the development of nuclear weapons).

When *Interrupted* was published in 2007, the nuclear issue was at the forefront of international politics—and it has never left. Iran has also drawn international attention over its disputed presidential elections in 2009,* the surprise election of Hassan Rouhani* in 2012, the unexpected improvements in US–Iran relations from 2013, and the signing of a nuclear agreement in 2015. These political developments make *Interrupted* enduringly topical and relevant to contemporary academic and political debates about Iran—but there is no evidence that the text has had an influence on policymakers.

Interaction

Interrupted stands as a direct challenge to orientalist* and neoconservative accounts of Iranian history, politics, and culture that Dabashi believes favor the West and stereotype everywhere else. He takes particular aim at historians and commentators such as Bernard Lewis,* Kenneth Pollack,* and Azar Nafisi* and their ideas. Dabashi is fiercely opposed to the kind of interventionist★ foreign policy these thinkers tend to like and also their depiction of Middle Eastern,

African, and Asian societies as being permanently caught between "tradition"* and "modernity."*

Interrupted was written when neoconservatives (who champion free-market economics and military intervention) held sway in the administration of President George W. Bush,* and they have played an active role in American politics ever since. Dabashi's ideas fit comfortably alongside a group of scholars including the late Edward Said,* the Lebanese American international relations scholar Fawaz Gerges,* the American historian Rashid Khalidi,* the international relations scholar John Mearsheimer,* and Stephen Walt,* a political scientist noted for developing the theoretical concept of "balance of threat," who challenge neoconservative foreign policy and orientalist interpretations of history.

However, it would be misleading to describe this group as being part of a specific school of thought. They work in different fields, ranging from postcolonial studies* to international relations theory. And while Dabashi's work fits in well within the intellectual environment, many of his contemporaries are more articulate in how they convey ideas and arguments.

The Continuing Debate

Hamid Dabashi and his work play a role in the academic and intellectual debates surrounding Iran. However, Dabashi's tendency to take unnecessary shots at authors he dislikes, his constant attacks on Israel, his inability to escape the jargon of academic theory, and his failure to communicate coherent arguments have left him isolated.

None of the people he attacks in *Interrupted* have made any attempt to respond so there has been no coordinated effort to challenge the work. Also, Dabashi's thesis relates specifically to how Iran's rich intellectual and literary traditions influence its anti-colonialist outlook. The subject is too narrowly academic to be part of mainstream arguments around international relations.

Nevertheless, the wider debate over Iran is highly polarized and often played out in the mass media. It pits neoconservatives and their "orientalist" allies, who want interventionist foreign policy in the Middle East, against liberals who call for diplomatic engagement instead.

Passions on both sides have run high since the election of Hassan Rouhani as Iranian president and the Obama* administration's public effort to win an agreement that scales back Iran's nuclear program and blocks all avenues to a bomb in exchange for sanctions relief. In the US, the neoconservatives and the pro-Israel lobby*—best represented by the commentator and diplomat John Bolton,* the international relations scholar Matthew Kroenig,* and more recently Senator Tom Cotton* of the right-wing Republican Party—have insisted the Obama administration takes a much harder line against Iran. Meanwhile the liberal camp—including the diplomat Thomas Pickering,* the Middle East analyst Gary Sick,* and the Iranian academic and lobbyist Trita Parsi*—advocate diplomatic engagement. This debate has played out very publically, particularly after the US reached an interim deal with Iran in November 2013, a framework in April 2015, and a comprehensive nuclear agreement in July 2015.

MODULE 12
WHERE NEXT?

KEY POINTS

* It is difficult to determine the long-term impact of *Iran: A People Interrupted,* though it is likely to have been hampered by Hamid Dabashi's jargon and personal attacks.

* *Iran: A People Interrupted* is a relatively new text so there has been no time for a school of thought to organize around Dabashi's arguments.

* The text is the first history in English to detail Iran's intellectual development, making it a landmark contribution to our understanding of Iranian literature.

Potential

Hamid Dabashi's *Iran: A People Interrupted* is undoubtedly an original and valuable account of a complex country. However, there are fundamental issues of style and content preventing it from reaching a wider audience or having a greater influence on contemporary debates about Iran.

The greatest obstacle to a higher profile for *Interrupted* is Dabashi's frequent reliance on dense, philosophical jargon. Highly complex prose makes it difficult for readers to follow his meaning. The work's academic impact is also diluted by the way Dabashi supplements literary history with attacks on the people he disagrees with and his claim to know more about Iran than the American government.

When he opens with "I promise you by the end of this book, you will know more about Iran than the U.S. Department of State, the CIA, the Pentagon ... all put together. I know things they do not know, or do not care to know, or would rather forget, or never learned,

> ❝Written into the very fabric of Iranian (and all other) national and nationalist historiography is a horrid patriarchal misogyny … If they are Arab, Azari, Baluchi, Kurd, Persian, Turkmen, or otherwise, they are all Iranian by virtue of their millennial struggle for women's rights, human rights, civil rights, for freedom and democracy, for decency, and for an abiding sense of justice. No dynastic history gave them that thriving and legitimate sense of dignity, no monarchy was needed to sustain it, and certainly no colonial or imperial hubris can take it away. ❞
>
> Hamid Dabashi, *Iran: A People Interrupted*

or would not tell you,"[1] one critic responded by describing *Interrupted* as "excessively opinionated," "pugnacious," "exasperating," and "reading almost like a rant."[2]

Frida Austvoll Nome,* a researcher at the Norwegian Institute of International Affairs, said the book suffered from Dabashi's "rudeness towards authors such as Bernard Lewis* and Azar Nafisi,"* which "significantly reduced the quality of this otherwise page-turning book."[3] As Nome highlights, the critical attention paid to Dabashi's controversial opinions and convoluted prose style obscures the fact that *Interrupted* is an illuminating study of Iran's intellectual history.

Future Directions

Dabashi's theoretical approach in *Interrupted* is inspired by the work of his late colleague and friend, Edward Said.* Said's *Orientalism* is an essential text in the field of postcolonial studies.* Supporters of Dabashi's work are writers and thinkers who share Said's theory that Western scholarship takes a condescending approach to other cultures. These scholars, including Rashid Khalidi* and the American Middle

East expert Juan Cole,* are deeply immersed in anti-colonial* scholarship through studying imperialism* and the politics of resistance. Like Dabashi, they take aim at the work of "orientalist"* scholars, with whom they disagree passionately.

In recent years, Cole has emerged as one of the more vocal opponents to orientalist views on foreign policy, particularly those put forward by Bernard Lewis in the aftermath of the 9/11* terror attacks on America. At this time, Lewis called for the United States to intervene militarily in the Middle East and sow the seeds of democracy* (the "Lewis Doctrine.") In an interview, Cole said that Lewis's call for "military intervention to transform failed Muslim states" risked escalating the clash between Islamic and Western cultures.[4] He was right.

Although the field of postcolonial studies has broadened since the death of Said in 2003, there is no evidence of anyone taking on or adapting Dabashi's highly intellectual, theoretical framework.[5] This is unfortunate as Dabashi's novel literary methodology could be applied to a variety of other countries with rich imperial and intellectual pasts, such as China, India, or Egypt.

While *Interrupted* is a spectacular study of Iran's literary history, rich with historical detail about Iran's intellectual and political elite, it will never have the same sweeping influence over scholarship as Said's *Orientalism*.

Summary

Interrupted is a brilliant analysis of the long relationship between literary and political life in Iran. As the first such study in the English language, the text makes a major contribution to international understanding of Iran's intellectual history. Dabashi offers an original overview of the Iranian people's resistance over 200 years to colonial* imperialism and internal tyranny. By revealing the complexity of this story he aims to discredit the Western idea that Iran is caught in a battle between tradition* and modernity.*

Unfortunately, Dabashi's achievements in *Interrupted* are weighed down by his radical stance on foreign policy and his caustic attacks on fellow thinkers. As a result, most reviews focus on these issues instead of his contribution to the study of Iran. Dabashi has not altered his style, however, and has gone on to publish numerous works that all employ a similar approach.[6]

While *Interrupted* is truly a significant text, Dabashi has become much more important than his book. His personal profile has grown through engaging in public debates about topical issues—mostly through his regular writing for news network Al Jazeera. Dabashi's role as a political commentator has proven to be much more important than the ideas contained in *Interrupted*, though the text remains as a useful and original contribution to the study of Iran.

NOTES

1   Hamid Dabashi, *Iran: A People Interrupted* (New York: The New Press, 2007), 11.

2   John Cappucci, review of *Iran: A People Interrupted*, by Hamid Dabashi, *International Journal of Middle Eastern Studies* 41, no. 3 (2009): 488–9.

3   Frida Austvoll Nome, review of *Iran: A People Interrupted*, by Hamid Dabashi, *Journal of Peace Research* 45, no. 2 (2008): 302.

4   Peter Waldman, "A Historian's Take on Islam Steers U.S. in Terrorism Fight," *Wall Street Journal*, February 3, 2004, accessed June 21, 2015, http://www.wsj.com/articles/SB107576070484918411.

5   "Members," PSA, accessed June 18, 2014, http://www.postcolonialstudiesassociation.co.uk/members/.

6   See Hamid Dabashi, *Islamic Liberation Theology: Resisting the Empire* (London: Routledge, 2009); *Iran, the Green Movement and the USA: The Fox and the Paradox* (London: Zed Books, 2010); *Shi'ism: A Religion of Protest* (Cambridge, MA: Belknap Press, 2011); *The Arab Spring: The End of Postcolonialism* (London: Zed Books, 2012); *Corpus Anarchicum: Political Protest, Suicidal Violence, and the Making of the Posthuman Body* (New York: Palgrave Macmillan, 2012).

GLOSSARY

GLOSSARY OF TERMS

Anti-imperialism: a political science and international relations concept used to explain any form of opposition to imperialism, colonialism, and empire.

Anti-Semitism: hostility or prejudice towards the Jewish people.

Apartheid: the official policy in South Africa between 1948 and 1991 of discrimination and segregation on the basis of race. The term comes from the Afrikaans for "separateness."

Arab Spring: a term used to describe a series of violent and non-violent protests, demonstrations, and civil wars that swept through the Arab world in 2010. As a result of the Arab Spring, rulers have been forced from power in Tunisia, Egypt, Libya, and Yemen, and civil wars have erupted and are continuing in Bahrain and Syria.

Axis of evil: term coined by US President George W. Bush in 2002 to refer to governments he believed were aiding terrorism, and specifically attacks against the West; these included Iran, Iraq and North Korea.

Ayatollah: a Shi'a religious leader. This is a title given to clerics who have become experts in areas of Islamic studies including jurisprudence, ethics, and philosophy, and who usually teach at Islamic seminaries.

Azerbaijan Crisis (1946–7): a Cold War crisis following World War II when the Soviet Union refused to withdraw its troops from Iran and then urged Iran's Azerbaijani and Kurdish citizens to declare independence. Iran took the matter to the United Nations, which condemned the Soviet Union's actions and forced it to withdraw.

Brookings Institution: an American think tank based in Washington, DC. It conducts research on economics, foreign policy, global economy, governance, and international development.

Charismatic authority: a concept that explains people's complete devotion to the exceptional heroism or exemplary character of an individual person, and the patterns they portray.

Civil disobedience: the conscious refusal to follow unjust laws on the basis that it is more just to break unjust laws than to obey them. It is used as a peaceful form of political protest.

Cold War (1947–91): period of tension between the United States and the Soviet Union that avoided direct military conflict, but was conducted through espionage and proxy wars.

Colonialism: refers to the rule of one country by another, involving unequal power relations between the ruler (colonist) and ruled (colony), and the exploitation of the colonies' resources to strengthen the economy of the colonizers' home country.

Communism: a political and social system in which major industries are owned and controlled by the state with one single party controlling all social, economic, and cultural aspects of society.

Constitutional Revolution (1905–11): a popular revolution that led to the establishment of a constitutional monarchy in Persia (Iran), including the creation of a constituent assembly. It is viewed as the point when Persia entered the modern era.

Decolonization: term referring to the period between 1946 and 1975 when European imperial powers granted independence to their colonial territories.

Democracy: a system of government where all the eligible members of a state participate equally in the election of representatives through regular elections.

Disputed Iran election (2009): the re-election of Mahmoud Ahmadinejad, who was accused of voter fraud, prompting widespread protests throughout Iran that were crushed violently.

Enlightenment: a Europe-wide intellectual movement that arose in the late seventeenth century. It put reason, rather than superstition or religion, at the heart of all human endeavors.

Green movement: a political movement that arose inside Iran following the disputed 2009 Iranian presidential election. Its central demand was the removal of President Mahmoud Ahmadinejad from office.

Historiography: the study of how a historical debate evolves over time.

Imperialism: a policy of extending a country's power and influence over other countries through the use of diplomacy or military force.

Interventionism: a position advocating a state using military or economic force to influence something that is not directly under its control.

Iran nuclear program: since the early 1990s Western powers have accused Iran of developing nuclear weapons. The Iranian government has maintained a right to develop peaceful nuclear technology and has denied having a nuclear weapons program. Negotiations about the issue have taken place periodically since 2003, leading to a comprehensive nuclear agreement in 2015.

Iranian Revolution (1978–9): a popular uprising in Iran that saw the overthrow of the Pahlavi dynasty and the Shah (king), Mohammad Reza Pahlavi, and the establishment of an Islamic republic, under the Ayatollah Ruhollah Khomeini.

Iraq War (2003–11): an armed conflict between the United States and Iraq. After toppling the government of Saddam Hussein in 2003, the conflict descended into a sectarian civil war that pitted Iraq's Shi'a and Sunni populations against each other. American forces withdrew from Iraq in December 2011.

Islamic Republic of Iran: formed in 1979 in the aftermath of the Iranian Revolution. It is a theocratic form of government (a government conducted on religious principles) led by a supreme jurist who ensures that all legislation abides by Islamic law.

Islamism: refers to a range of ideologies that view Islam as a source of social and political guidance.

Israel lobby: a grouping of individuals and organizations working to maximize Israel's influence over the direction of American foreign policy in the Middle East.

Karbala, Battle of: battle between Sunni and Shi'a armies in 680 C.E. that resulted in the death of Imam Ali, whom Shi'as revere and regard as a martyr.

Khariji: a group of Muslims who initially supported the Shi'a following the Prophet Mohammad's death but later turned against the Imam Ali. They insisted that any Muslim could be a leader of the Muslim community and had the right to revolt against any ruler who deviated from their interpretation of Islam.

McCarthyism: a period of political repression in the United States lasting roughly from 1950 to 1957 and named after Senator Joseph McCarthy. Also called the Red Scare, it tried to root out communists, especially those who might be spying for the Soviet Union. The term is often used today to mean a process of making allegations against individuals for political repression and control.

Modernity: relates to the modern era, where traditional or feudal values have been replaced by enlightened values.

Nationalism: a belief, creed, or political ideology that involves individuals identifying with, or becoming attached to, their nation.

Neoconservatism: an American political movement that emphasizes proactive promotion of free markets and the aggressive promotion of democracy via military force.

9/11: the name given to a series of terrorist attacks on New York City and Washington, DC on September 11, 2001. The attacks, orchestrated by the militant Islamist group al-Qaeda, killed around 3,000 people.

Orientalism: a concept referring to the general patronizing nature of Western attitudes towards Middle Eastern, Asian, and North African societies.

Pahlavi Dynasty: the rule of Reza Shah Pahlavi (1878–1944), who became king in a coup in 1925 and was overthrown by the British and Russians in 1941, and that of his son Mohammad Reza Pahlavi (1919–80), who ruled from 1941 until his overthrow in 1979.

Postcolonialism: an academic discipline established in the early 1960s that focuses on analyzing intellectual discourses between colonial powers and those whom they colonize in order to analyze, explain, and respond to the legacies of both colonialism and imperialism.

SAVAK (Organization of Intelligence and National Security): Iran's former secret police and intelligence service.

Shi'a/Shi'ism/Shi'ite: one of the two main branches of Islam; it broke from the majority Sunni sect following the death of the Prophet Muhammad in 632 C.E. The dominant religion inside Iran, its followers reject the first three Sunni caliphs and regard the Imam Ali, the fourth caliph, as Muhammad's first true successor.

Socialism: the belief that society should be organized in such a way that the methods of production, distribution, and exchange are owned and regulated by the community as a whole, rather than by the privileged few.

Soviet Union, or USSR: a kind of "super state" that existed from 1922 to 1991, centered primarily on Russia and its neighbors in Eastern Europe and the northern half of Asia. It was the communist pole of the Cold War, with the United States as its main "rival."

Sunni: the most popular branch of Islam, with roughly 90 percent of Muslims identifying with this sect. It differs from Shi'ism through its acceptance of the first three caliphs, following the Prophet Muhammad's death.

Tradition: a long-established custom or belief or the passing of customs or beliefs from generation to generation.

War on Terror: a term often applied to the American-led military campaign against terrorist groups involved in the 9/11 terrorist attacks on the United States.

White Revolution: a series of reforms in Iran that were launched in 1963 by the Shah (king), Mohammad Reza Pahlavi, and which were designed to transform Iran into a modern industrial state, while limiting the power of the Iranian aristocracy and the religious establishment.

PEOPLE MENTIONED IN THE TEXT

Kaveh Afrasiabi (b. 1968) is an Iranian American political scientist and author.

Mahmoud Ahmadinejad (b. 1956) is an Iranian politician who was the sixth president of Iran from 2005 to 2013. His two terms in office were noted for the rapid expansion of Iran's nuclear program that took place and for his anti-Semitic (that is, showing hostility to Jewish people) speeches.

Michael Axworthy (b. 1962) is a British academic, author, and political commentator who served as the head of the Iran section at the British Foreign and Commonwealth Office between 1998 and 2000. He is most noted for his studies of Iranian history, notably *Revolutionary Iran* (2013) and *Empire of the Mind* (2007).

John Bolton (b. 1948) is a neoconservative commentator and diplomat, who served as the US ambassador to the United Nations from August 2005 until December 2006.

George W. Bush (b. 1946) was the 43rd President of the United States. He served two terms, from 2001 to 2009.

John Cappucci is a doctoral candidate in the department of political science at Carleton University in Ottawa. He studies the Middle East.

Dipesh Chakrabarty (b. 1948) is a Bengali historian and postcolonial theorist. He is a member of the subaltern studies group, which focuses on the historical experience of persons who are politically, culturally, and geographically outside dominant power structures.

Juan Cole (b. 1952) is an American political commentator and academic at the University of Michigan, who focuses primarily on the Middle East. He also runs a syndicated blog, *Informed Content*.

Tom Cotton (b. 1977) is an American politician and the junior United States senator from Arkansas for the Republican Party. He gained prominence after drafting a letter to the Iranian government lecturing it on the US constitution.

Frantz Fanon (1925–61) was a Martinique-born French psychiatrist, philosopher, and revolutionary who fought for the independence of Algeria in the Algerian War (1954–62). His text *Black Skin, White Masks* (1952) laid the intellectual foundation for the field of postcolonial studies.

Benjamin Franklin (1706–90) was an American statesman, philosopher, inventor, and scientist best known for his part in the drafting of the United States Declaration of Independence (1776), his formulation of a theory of electricity, and his famous demonstration of the electrical nature of lightning.

Francis Fukuyama (b. 1952) is an American political scientist, political economist, and author.

Robert Fulford (b. 1932) is a Canadian journalist, magazine editor, and essayist who writes regularly for the *National Post*, a conservative Canadian newspaper.

Clifford Geertz (1926–2006) was a professor of anthropology at Princeton University, best known for his work in cultural anthropology. His work was particularly concerned with conceptualizing the role of symbols in cultural contexts.

Fawaz Gerges (b. 1958) is a Lebanese-born American academic and author who has published numerous books dealing with the Middle East, US foreign policy, terrorism, and the Western world's relations with Islam. He is a professor of international relations at the London School of Economics.

Johann Wolfgang von Goethe (1749–1832) was a German poet, playwright, novelist, philosopher, and scientist, best known for his play *Faust*.

Jürgen Habermas (b. 1929) is a German social philosopher. He is a leading figure of the Frankfurt school of philosophy. He developed its cultural reappraisal of Marxism and is especially noted for his work on communication theory.

Samuel Huntington (1927–2008) was professor of international relations at Harvard University from 1963 until his death. His book *The Clash of Civilizations and the Remaking of World Order* (1996) is widely considered the most influential post-Cold War analysis of international order.

Ron Jacobs is an American political commentator and writer.

Rashid Khalidi (b. 1948) is an American historian of the Middle East. As well as his role as director of the Middle East Institute of Columbia's School of International and Public Affairs, he also serves as editor of the *Journal of Palestine Studies*.

Ruhollah Mousavi Khomeini (1902–89) was an Iranian Shi'ite Muslim leader and the founder of the Islamic Republic of Iran; he first emerged as an opposition leader to Shah Mohammad Reza Pahlavi in 1963 and became the symbol for resistance during the Iranian Revolution. After returning from exile in 1979, he established Iran as a fundamentalist Islamic republic and relentlessly pursued the Iran–Iraq War of 1980–8.

Matthew Kroenig is an associate professor of international relations in the Department of Government at Georgetown University.

Bernard Lewis (b. 1916) is a neoconservative British American historian, public intellectual, and political commentator.

Karl Mannheim (1893–1947) was a Hungarian-born sociologist now widely considered one of the founding fathers of classical sociology and the sociology of knowledge.

John Mearsheimer (b. 1947) is a professor of international relations at the University of Chicago and a leading international relations theorist from the neorealist school of political thought. He developed the theory of offensive realism.

Abbas Milani (b. 1949) is the Hamid & Christina Moghadam Director of Iranian Studies at Stanford University and a professor (by courtesy) in the Division of Stanford Global Studies. He was a founder of the Iran Democracy Project and a research fellow at the Hoover Institution. His areas of expertise are US–Iran relations and Iranian cultural, political, and security issues.

Mohammad Mossadeq (1882–1967) was Iran's democratically elected prime minister between 1951 and 1953, the year in which he was overthrown in a CIA-sponsored coup. He was a fierce Iranian nationalist who was dedicated to removing British influence from Iran and its control over Iran's oil resources.

Azar Nafisi (b. 1955) is an Iranian writer and professor of English literature. She is best known for her book *Reading Lolita in Tehran*.

Frida Austvoll Nome is a researcher at the Norwegian Institute of International Affairs.

Barack Obama (b. 1961) is the 44th president of the United States and was elected in 2008. He is the country's first black president.

Mohammad Reza Pahlavi (1919–80) was the Shah (king) of Iran from September 1941 until he was overthrown by a popular uprising in 1979. He fled the country in February 1979 and died from cancer the following year. He was a close ally of the United States during the Cold War.

Trita Parsi (b. 1974) is an Iranian academic, author, and founder and current president of the National Iranian American Council.

Thomas Pickering (b. 1931) is an American diplomat who has served as a United States ambassador on five separate occasions, including a term as Ambassador to the United Nations from 1989 to 1992.

Kenneth Pollack (b. 1966), a former Central Intelligence Agency (CIA) intelligence analyst, is a National Security Staff member and an expert on Middle East politics and military affairs at the Brookings Institute.

Nasir al-Din Shah Qajar (1831–96) was the King (Shah) of Persia from 1848 to 1896.

Hassan Rouhani (b. 1948) is the seventh president of Iran, a Muslim cleric, lawyer, academic, and former diplomat. He was elected in 2013.

Sa'di (1210–91/2) was a Persian poet, famous not only in Iran but around the world. In his works *Bostan* (*The Orchard*) and *Gulistan* (*The Rose Garden*) he preached values like justice, liberty, modesty, and contentment.

Edward Said (1935–2003) was a Palestinian literary theorist, critic, journalist, and pro-Palestinian activist. He is best known for his book *Orientalism* (1978), which was a critique of the generally patronizing nature of Western attitudes towards Middle Eastern, Asian, and North African societies.

Jean-Paul Sartre (1905–80) was a French philosopher who was a prominent figure in the development of the existential school of philosophy. In *Being and Nothingness* (1943), he examined the concepts of phenomenology and ontology (the nature of being).

Mirza Saleh Shirazi established the first newspaper in Iran in 1837 and devised a simplified form of Persian, which allowed ordinary Iranians to learn to read.

Gary Sick (b. 1935) is professor of international affairs at Columbia University, and a recognized analyst of Middle East affairs with special expertise on Iran. He served on the staff of the National Security Council under three US presidents—Ford, Carter, and Reagan.

Gayatri Chakravorty Spivak (b. 1942) is a renowned theorist in the field of postcolonialism. She is known for her political use of feminist, Marxist, deconstructionist theories (very roughly, theories founded on the principle that, given the role of language in constructing "reality," it is difficult to arrive at objective truth) to question colonialism and the way we have been conditioned to think about literature.

Joseph Stalin (1878–1953) was the leader of the Soviet Union from the mid-1920s until his death in 1953. He is best known for his ruthless authoritarian style of rule, notably his campaign against the Soviet intelligentsia between 1936 and 1939 when hundreds of thousands were executed.

Henry David Thoreau (1817–62) was an American essayist and poet, best known for his essay *Civil Disobedience* (1849), which influenced the policy of passive resistance adopted by Mahatma Gandhi (1869–1948).

Voltaire (1694–1778) was a pseudonym of François-Marie Arouet, a French writer, playwright, and poet. He was a leading figure of the Enlightenment and frequently came into conflict with the establishment because of his radical views and satirical writings.

Stephen Walt (b. 1955) is a professor of international relations at Harvard University and a leading international relations theorist from the neorealist school of political thought. He developed the theoretical concept known as "balance of threat."

Max Weber (1864–1920) was a German sociologist and philosopher whose concept of dialectics—which points out contradictions between two objects/groups—has had a profound impact on the study of philosophy, particularly Marxism.

WORKS CITED

WORKS CITED

Afrasiabi, Kaveh. "Pseudo-Intellectualism on Iran: Review: *Iran: A People Interrupted*, by Hamid Dabashi." *Asia Times*, November 15, 2008.

Cappucci, John. Review of *Iran: A People Interrupted*, by Hamid Dabashi. *International Journal of Middle Eastern Studies* 41, no. 3 (2009): 488–9.

Chelkowski, Peter, and Hamid Dabashi. *Staging a Revolution: The Art of Persuasion in the Islamic Republic of Iran*. New York: New York University Press, 2002.

Dabashi, Hamid. *Authority in Islam: From the Rise of Muhammad to the Establishment of the Umayyads*. New Brunswick, NJ: Transaction Publishers, 1989.

———. *Truth and Narrative: The Untimely Thoughts of 'Ayn al-Qudat al-Hamadhani*. London: Curzon Press, 1999.

———. *Close Up: Iranian Cinema, Past, Present and Future*. New York: Verso, 2001.

———. *Theology of Discontent: The Ideological Foundation of the Islamic Revolution in Iran*. New Brunswick, NJ: Transaction Publishers, 2005.

———. "Native Informers and the Making of the American Empire." *Al-Ahram Weekly* 797, no. 1 (June 2006).

———. *Iran: A People Interrupted*. New York: The New Press, 2007.

———. *Masters and Masterpieces of Iranian Cinema*. New York: Mage, 2007.

———. *Post-Orientalism: Knowledge and Power in Time of Terror*. New Brunswick, NJ: Transaction Publishers, 2008.

———. *Islamic Liberation Theology: Resisting the Empire*. London: Routledge, 2009.

———. *Iran, the Green Movement and the USA: The Fox and the Paradox*. London: Zed Books, 2010.

———. *The Green Movement in Iran*. New Brunswick, NJ: Transaction Publishers, 2011.

———. *Shi'ism: A Religion of Protest*. Cambridge, MA: Belknap Press, 2011.

———. *The Arab Spring: The End of Postcolonialism*. London: Zed Books, 2012.

———. *Corpus Anarchicum: Political Protest, Suicidal Violence, and the Making of the Posthuman Body*. New York: Palgrave Macmillan, 2012.

Dodge, Toby. *Iraq: From War to a New Authoritarianism*. London: Routledge, 2013.

Esmaeli, Kouross. Review of *Iran: A People Interrupted*, by Hamid Dabashi.

Comparative Studies of South Asia, Africa and the Middle East 28, no. 2 (2008): 375.

Fukuyama, Francis. *The End of History and the Last Man*. New York: Free Press, 2006.

Fulford, Robert. "Reading Lolita at Columbia." *National Post*, November 6, 2006.

Huntington, Samuel. *The Clash of Civilizations and the Remaking of World Order.* New York: Simon & Schuster, 1996.

Jacobs, Ron. "Transcending the Colonizer's History." A Review of *Iran: A People Interrupted*, by Hamid Dabashi. *OpEd News*, January 1, 2008.

Mearsheimer, John J., and Stephen M. Walt. *The Israel Lobby and US Foreign Policy.* New York: Farrar, Straus and Giroux, 2007.

Nafisi, Azar. *Reading Lolita in Tehran: A Memoir in Books*. New York: Random House, 2003.

Nasr, Seyyed Hossein, and Oliver Leaman, eds. *History of Islamic Philosophy.* London: Routledge, 1996.

Nome, Frida Austvoll. Review of *Iran: A People Interrupted*, by Hamid Dabashi. *Journal of Peace Research* 45, no. 2 (2008): 302.

Pollack, Kenneth. *The Threatening Storm: The Case for Invading Iraq.* New York: Random House, 2002.

———. *The Persian Puzzle: The Conflict between Iran and America*. New York: Random House, 2005.Ricks, Thomas E. *Fiasco: The American Military Adventure in Iraq*. New York: Penguin, 2006.

———. *The Gamble: General David Petraeus and the American Military Adventure in Iraq, 2006–2008*. New York: Penguin, 2009.

Rosenthal, Keith. "Correcting Western Views of Iran." Review of *Iran: A People Interrupted*, by Hamid Dabashi. *International Socialist Review* 55 (2007).

Rubin, Michael. Review of *The Green Movement in Iran*, by Hamid Dabashi. *Middle East Quarterly* 19, no. 3 (2012): 89–90.

Said, Edward. *Orientalism*. New York: Vintage Books, 1978.

Schwartz, Stephen. Review of *Islamic Liberation Theology*, by Hamid Dabashi. *Middle East Quarterly* 16, no. 1 (2009): 84.

Weiss, John. Review of *Iran: A People Interrupted*, by Hamid Dabashi. *Talk With Iran*, December 10, 2007.

THE MACAT LIBRARY
BY DISCIPLINE

AFRICANA STUDIES

Chinua Achebe's *An Image of Africa: Racism in Conrad's Heart of Darkness*
W. E. B. Du Bois's *The Souls of Black Folk*
Zora Neale Huston's *Characteristics of Negro Expression*
Martin Luther King Jr's *Why We Can't Wait*
Toni Morrison's *Playing in the Dark: Whiteness in the American Literary Imagination*

ANTHROPOLOGY

Arjun Appadurai's *Modernity at Large: Cultural Dimensions of Globalisation*
Philippe Ariès's *Centuries of Childhood*
Franz Boas's *Race, Language and Culture*
Kim Chan & Renée Mauborgne's *Blue Ocean Strategy*
Jared Diamond's *Guns, Germs & Steel: the Fate of Human Societies*
Jared Diamond's *Collapse: How Societies Choose to Fail or Survive*
E. E. Evans-Pritchard's *Witchcraft, Oracles and Magic Among the Azande*
James Ferguson's *The Anti-Politics Machine*
Clifford Geertz's *The Interpretation of Cultures*
David Graeber's *Debt: the First 5000 Years*
Karen Ho's *Liquidated: An Ethnography of Wall Street*
Geert Hofstede's *Culture's Consequences: Comparing Values, Behaviors, Institutes and Organizations across Nations*
Claude Lévi-Strauss's *Structural Anthropology*
Jay Macleod's *Ain't No Makin' It: Aspirations and Attainment in a Low-Income Neighborhood*
Saba Mahmood's *The Politics of Piety: The Islamic Revival and the Feminist Subject*
Marcel Mauss's *The Gift*

BUSINESS

Jean Lave & Etienne Wenger's *Situated Learning*
Theodore Levitt's *Marketing Myopia*
Burton G. Malkiel's *A Random Walk Down Wall Street*
Douglas McGregor's *The Human Side of Enterprise*
Michael Porter's *Competitive Strategy: Creating and Sustaining Superior Performance*
John Kotter's *Leading Change*
C. K. Prahalad & Gary Hamel's *The Core Competence of the Corporation*

CRIMINOLOGY

Michelle Alexander's *The New Jim Crow: Mass Incarceration in the Age of Colorblindness*
Michael R. Gottfredson & Travis Hirschi's *A General Theory of Crime*
Richard Herrnstein & Charles A. Murray's *The Bell Curve: Intelligence and Class Structure in American Life*
Elizabeth Loftus's *Eyewitness Testimony*
Jay Macleod's *Ain't No Makin' It: Aspirations and Attainment in a Low-Income Neighborhood*
Philip Zimbardo's *The Lucifer Effect*

ECONOMICS

Janet Abu-Lughod's *Before European Hegemony*
Ha-Joon Chang's *Kicking Away the Ladder*
David Brion Davis's *The Problem of Slavery in the Age of Revolution*
Milton Friedman's *The Role of Monetary Policy*
Milton Friedman's *Capitalism and Freedom*
David Graeber's *Debt: the First 5000 Years*
Friedrich Hayek's *The Road to Serfdom*
Karen Ho's *Liquidated: An Ethnography of Wall Street*

John Maynard Keynes's *The General Theory of Employment, Interest and Money*
Charles P. Kindleberger's *Manias, Panics and Crashes*
Robert Lucas's *Why Doesn't Capital Flow from Rich to Poor Countries?*
Burton G. Malkiel's *A Random Walk Down Wall Street*
Thomas Robert Malthus's *An Essay on the Principle of Population*
Karl Marx's *Capital*
Thomas Piketty's *Capital in the Twenty-First Century*
Amartya Sen's *Development as Freedom*
Adam Smith's *The Wealth of Nations*
Nassim Nicholas Taleb's *The Black Swan: The Impact of the Highly Improbable*
Amos Tversky's & Daniel Kahneman's *Judgment under Uncertainty: Heuristics and Biases*
Mahbub Ul Haq's *Reflections on Human Development*
Max Weber's *The Protestant Ethic and the Spirit of Capitalism*

FEMINISM AND GENDER STUDIES

Judith Butler's *Gender Trouble*
Simone De Beauvoir's *The Second Sex*
Michel Foucault's *History of Sexuality*
Betty Friedan's *The Feminine Mystique*
Saba Mahmood's *The Politics of Piety: The Islamic Revival and the Feminist Subject*
Joan Wallach Scott's *Gender and the Politics of History*
Mary Wollstonecraft's *A Vindication of the Rights of Women*
Virginia Woolf's *A Room of One's Own*

GEOGRAPHY

The Brundtland Report's *Our Common Future*
Rachel Carson's *Silent Spring*
Charles Darwin's *On the Origin of Species*
James Ferguson's *The Anti-Politics Machine*
Jane Jacobs's *The Death and Life of Great American Cities*
James Lovelock's *Gaia: A New Look at Life on Earth*
Amartya Sen's *Development as Freedom*
Mathis Wackernagel & William Rees's *Our Ecological Footprint*

HISTORY

Janet Abu-Lughod's *Before European Hegemony*
Benedict Anderson's *Imagined Communities*
Bernard Bailyn's *The Ideological Origins of the American Revolution*
Hanna Batatu's *The Old Social Classes And The Revolutionary Movements Of Iraq*
Christopher Browning's *Ordinary Men: Reserve Police Batallion 101 and the Final Solution in Poland*
Edmund Burke's *Reflections on the Revolution in France*
William Cronon's *Nature's Metropolis: Chicago And The Great West*
Alfred W. Crosby's *The Columbian Exchange*
Hamid Dabashi's *Iran: A People Interrupted*
David Brion Davis's *The Problem of Slavery in the Age of Revolution*
Nathalie Zemon Davis's *The Return of Martin Guerre*
Jared Diamond's *Guns, Germs & Steel: the Fate of Human Societies*
Frank Dikotter's *Mao's Great Famine*
John W Dower's *War Without Mercy: Race And Power In The Pacific War*
W. E. B. Du Bois's *The Souls of Black Folk*
Richard J. Evans's *In Defence of History*
Lucien Febvre's *The Problem of Unbelief in the 16th Century*
Sheila Fitzpatrick's *Everyday Stalinism*

The Macat Library By Discipline

Eric Foner's *Reconstruction: America's Unfinished Revolution, 1863-1877*
Michel Foucault's *Discipline and Punish*
Michel Foucault's *History of Sexuality*
Francis Fukuyama's *The End of History and the Last Man*
John Lewis Gaddis's *We Now Know: Rethinking Cold War History*
Ernest Gellner's *Nations and Nationalism*
Eugene Genovese's *Roll, Jordan, Roll: The World the Slaves Made*
Carlo Ginzburg's *The Night Battles*
Daniel Goldhagen's *Hitler's Willing Executioners*
Jack Goldstone's *Revolution and Rebellion in the Early Modern World*
Antonio Gramsci's *The Prison Notebooks*
Alexander Hamilton, John Jay & James Madison's *The Federalist Papers*
Christopher Hill's *The World Turned Upside Down*
Carole Hillenbrand's *The Crusades: Islamic Perspectives*
Thomas Hobbes's *Leviathan*
Eric Hobsbawm's *The Age Of Revolution*
John A. Hobson's *Imperialism: A Study*
Albert Hourani's *History of the Arab Peoples*
Samuel P. Huntington's *The Clash of Civilizations and the Remaking of World Order*
C. L. R. James's *The Black Jacobins*
Tony Judt's *Postwar: A History of Europe Since 1945*
Ernst Kantorowicz's *The King's Two Bodies: A Study in Medieval Political Theology*
Paul Kennedy's *The Rise and Fall of the Great Powers*
Ian Kershaw's *The "Hitler Myth": Image and Reality in the Third Reich*
John Maynard Keynes's *The General Theory of Employment, Interest and Money*
Charles P. Kindleberger's *Manias, Panics and Crashes*
Martin Luther King Jr's *Why We Can't Wait*
Henry Kissinger's *World Order: Reflections on the Character of Nations and the Course of History*
Thomas Kuhn's *The Structure of Scientific Revolutions*
Georges Lefebvre's *The Coming of the French Revolution*
John Locke's *Two Treatises of Government*
Niccolò Machiavelli's *The Prince*
Thomas Robert Malthus's *An Essay on the Principle of Population*
Mahmood Mamdani's *Citizen and Subject: Contemporary Africa And The Legacy Of Late Colonialism*
Karl Marx's *Capital*
Stanley Milgram's *Obedience to Authority*
John Stuart Mill's *On Liberty*
Thomas Paine's *Common Sense*
Thomas Paine's *Rights of Man*
Geoffrey Parker's *Global Crisis: War, Climate Change and Catastrophe in the Seventeenth Century*
Jonathan Riley-Smith's *The First Crusade and the Idea of Crusading*
Jean-Jacques Rousseau's *The Social Contract*
Joan Wallach Scott's *Gender and the Politics of History*
Theda Skocpol's *States and Social Revolutions*
Adam Smith's *The Wealth of Nations*
Timothy Snyder's *Bloodlands: Europe Between Hitler and Stalin*
Sun Tzu's *The Art of War*
Keith Thomas's *Religion and the Decline of Magic*
Thucydides's *The History of the Peloponnesian War*
Frederick Jackson Turner's *The Significance of the Frontier in American History*
Odd Arne Westad's *The Global Cold War: Third World Interventions And The Making Of Our Times*

LITERATURE

Chinua Achebe's *An Image of Africa: Racism in Conrad's Heart of Darkness*
Roland Barthes's *Mythologies*
Homi K. Bhabha's *The Location of Culture*
Judith Butler's *Gender Trouble*
Simone De Beauvoir's *The Second Sex*
Ferdinand De Saussure's *Course in General Linguistics*
T. S. Eliot's *The Sacred Wood: Essays on Poetry and Criticism*
Zora Neale Huston's *Characteristics of Negro Expression*
Toni Morrison's *Playing in the Dark: Whiteness in the American Literary Imagination*
Edward Said's *Orientalism*
Gayatri Chakravorty Spivak's *Can the Subaltern Speak?*
Mary Wollstonecraft's *A Vindication of the Rights of Women*
Virginia Woolf's *A Room of One's Own*

PHILOSOPHY

Elizabeth Anscombe's *Modern Moral Philosophy*
Hannah Arendt's *The Human Condition*
Aristotle's *Metaphysics*
Aristotle's *Nicomachean Ethics*
Edmund Gettier's *Is Justified True Belief Knowledge?*
Georg Wilhelm Friedrich Hegel's *Phenomenology of Spirit*
David Hume's *Dialogues Concerning Natural Religion*
David Hume's *The Enquiry for Human Understanding*
Immanuel Kant's *Religion within the Boundaries of Mere Reason*
Immanuel Kant's *Critique of Pure Reason*
Søren Kierkegaard's *The Sickness Unto Death*
Søren Kierkegaard's *Fear and Trembling*
C. S. Lewis's *The Abolition of Man*
Alasdair MacIntyre's *After Virtue*
Marcus Aurelius's *Meditations*
Friedrich Nietzsche's *On the Genealogy of Morality*
Friedrich Nietzsche's *Beyond Good and Evil*
Plato's *Republic*
Plato's *Symposium*
Jean-Jacques Rousseau's *The Social Contract*
Gilbert Ryle's *The Concept of Mind*
Baruch Spinoza's *Ethics*
Sun Tzu's *The Art of War*
Ludwig Wittgenstein's *Philosophical Investigations*

POLITICS

Benedict Anderson's *Imagined Communities*
Aristotle's *Politics*
Bernard Bailyn's *The Ideological Origins of the American Revolution*
Edmund Burke's *Reflections on the Revolution in France*
John C. Calhoun's *A Disquisition on Government*
Ha-Joon Chang's *Kicking Away the Ladder*
Hamid Dabashi's *Iran: A People Interrupted*
Hamid Dabashi's *Theology of Discontent: The Ideological Foundation of the Islamic Revolution in Iran*
Robert Dahl's *Democracy and its Critics*
Robert Dahl's *Who Governs?*
David Brion Davis's *The Problem of Slavery in the Age of Revolution*

The Macat Library By Discipline

Alexis De Tocqueville's *Democracy in America*
James Ferguson's *The Anti-Politics Machine*
Frank Dikotter's *Mao's Great Famine*
Sheila Fitzpatrick's *Everyday Stalinism*
Eric Foner's *Reconstruction: America's Unfinished Revolution, 1863-1877*
Milton Friedman's *Capitalism and Freedom*
Francis Fukuyama's *The End of History and the Last Man*
John Lewis Gaddis's *We Now Know: Rethinking Cold War History*
Ernest Gellner's *Nations and Nationalism*
David Graeber's *Debt: the First 5000 Years*
Antonio Gramsci's *The Prison Notebooks*
Alexander Hamilton, John Jay & James Madison's *The Federalist Papers*
Friedrich Hayek's *The Road to Serfdom*
Christopher Hill's *The World Turned Upside Down*
Thomas Hobbes's *Leviathan*
John A. Hobson's *Imperialism: A Study*
Samuel P. Huntington's *The Clash of Civilizations and the Remaking of World Order*
Tony Judt's *Postwar: A History of Europe Since 1945*
David C. Kang's *China Rising: Peace, Power and Order in East Asia*
Paul Kennedy's *The Rise and Fall of Great Powers*
Robert Keohane's *After Hegemony*
Martin Luther King Jr.'s *Why We Can't Wait*
Henry Kissinger's *World Order: Reflections on the Character of Nations and the Course of History*
John Locke's *Two Treatises of Government*
Niccolò Machiavelli's *The Prince*
Thomas Robert Malthus's *An Essay on the Principle of Population*
Mahmood Mamdani's *Citizen and Subject: Contemporary Africa And The Legacy Of Late Colonialism*
Karl Marx's *Capital*
John Stuart Mill's *On Liberty*
John Stuart Mill's *Utilitarianism*
Hans Morgenthau's *Politics Among Nations*
Thomas Paine's *Common Sense*
Thomas Paine's *Rights of Man*
Thomas Piketty's *Capital in the Twenty-First Century*
Robert D. Putman's *Bowling Alone*
John Rawls's *Theory of Justice*
Jean-Jacques Rousseau's *The Social Contract*
Theda Skocpol's *States and Social Revolutions*
Adam Smith's *The Wealth of Nations*
Sun Tzu's *The Art of War*
Henry David Thoreau's *Civil Disobedience*
Thucydides's *The History of the Peloponnesian War*
Kenneth Waltz's *Theory of International Politics*
Max Weber's *Politics as a Vocation*
Odd Arne Westad's *The Global Cold War: Third World Interventions And The Making Of Our Times*

POSTCOLONIAL STUDIES

Roland Barthes's *Mythologies*
Frantz Fanon's *Black Skin, White Masks*
Homi K. Bhabha's *The Location of Culture*
Gustavo Gutiérrez's *A Theology of Liberation*
Edward Said's *Orientalism*
Gayatri Chakravorty Spivak's *Can the Subaltern Speak?*

PSYCHOLOGY

Gordon Allport's *The Nature of Prejudice*
Alan Baddeley & Graham Hitch's *Aggression: A Social Learning Analysis*
Albert Bandura's *Aggression: A Social Learning Analysis*
Leon Festinger's *A Theory of Cognitive Dissonance*
Sigmund Freud's *The Interpretation of Dreams*
Betty Friedan's *The Feminine Mystique*
Michael R. Gottfredson & Travis Hirschi's *A General Theory of Crime*
Eric Hoffer's *The True Believer: Thoughts on the Nature of Mass Movements*
William James's *Principles of Psychology*
Elizabeth Loftus's *Eyewitness Testimony*
A. H. Maslow's *A Theory of Human Motivation*
Stanley Milgram's *Obedience to Authority*
Steven Pinker's *The Better Angels of Our Nature*
Oliver Sacks's *The Man Who Mistook His Wife For a Hat*
Richard Thaler & Cass Sunstein's *Nudge: Improving Decisions About Health, Wealth and Happiness*
Amos Tversky's *Judgment under Uncertainty: Heuristics and Biases*
Philip Zimbardo's *The Lucifer Effect*

SCIENCE

Rachel Carson's *Silent Spring*
William Cronon's *Nature's Metropolis: Chicago And The Great West*
Alfred W. Crosby's *The Columbian Exchange*
Charles Darwin's *On the Origin of Species*
Richard Dawkin's *The Selfish Gene*
Thomas Kuhn's *The Structure of Scientific Revolutions*
Geoffrey Parker's *Global Crisis: War, Climate Change and Catastrophe in the Seventeenth Century*
Mathis Wackernagel & William Rees's *Our Ecological Footprint*

SOCIOLOGY

Michelle Alexander's *The New Jim Crow: Mass Incarceration in the Age of Colorblindness*
Gordon Allport's *The Nature of Prejudice*
Albert Bandura's *Aggression: A Social Learning Analysis*
Hanna Batatu's *The Old Social Classes And The Revolutionary Movements Of Iraq*
Ha-Joon Chang's *Kicking Away the Ladder*
W. E. B. Du Bois's *The Souls of Black Folk*
Émile Durkheim's *On Suicide*
Frantz Fanon's *Black Skin, White Masks*
Frantz Fanon's *The Wretched of the Earth*
Eric Foner's *Reconstruction: America's Unfinished Revolution, 1863-1877*
Eugene Genovese's *Roll, Jordan, Roll: The World the Slaves Made*
Jack Goldstone's *Revolution and Rebellion in the Early Modern World*
Antonio Gramsci's *The Prison Notebooks*
Richard Herrnstein & Charles A Murray's *The Bell Curve: Intelligence and Class Structure in American Life*
Eric Hoffer's *The True Believer: Thoughts on the Nature of Mass Movements*
Jane Jacobs's *The Death and Life of Great American Cities*
Robert Lucas's *Why Doesn't Capital Flow from Rich to Poor Countries?*
Jay Macleod's *Ain't No Makin' It: Aspirations and Attainment in a Low Income Neighborhood*
Elaine May's *Homeward Bound: American Families in the Cold War Era*
Douglas McGregor's *The Human Side of Enterprise*
C. Wright Mills's *The Sociological Imagination*